WHAT IS BABYLON?

"So he carried me away in the Spirit into the wilderness: and I saw a woman sit upon a scarlet colored beast.

"And upon her forehead was a name written, MYSTERY, BABYLON, THE GREAT, THE MOTHER OF HARLOTS AND ABOMINATIONS OF THE EARTH."

—Rev. 17:3-5.

By

J. F. LAWSON

E. E. Byrum's Vision

In about 1932, Brother Byrum told me a vision he had. He said he was in his home one afternoon resting. (Many know its location on the Anderson, Ind. camp grounds.) He said, "I know I was not asleep. A vision appeared to me. As I looked across the deep draw, which was between my home and the school dormitory, I saw in my vision, buildings where the dormitory stood, and a ladder extending from the ground and leading up to an entrance into this building. But the ladder was not directly connected to the building, but was hooked into Brother D. O. Teasley's vest pockets. There was a goodly number of people ascending this ladder to the entrance of this building. There was a rather short man from the west, just inside this building with a machine, which he said would lead to greater success in getting people into the church of God. And there were guides leading the people through the building. I went over and went up to see and to hear what the man with the machine had to say. But when I went in, they told me to pass on; so I went out and went to the old tabernacle and it was full of people. A man with this machine was explaining its wonders to the audience. I heard moaning and groaning under the rostrum; I looked and the old ministers were under there praying. A sudden crash and this machine fell to the floor so twisted and wrecked that it never could be repaired." (Given by Bro. D. E. Nelson.)

It was in 1917, that D. O. Teasley was general manager of the Gospel Trumpet Company, and the whole system of operation was changed from consecrated labor to paid salaries, based on wages in the commercial world. This opened the door for organization, in which the man mentioned above, seemed to be the key man in its promotion. This machine was soon set up in the General Assemblies over in the old auditorium, and has been runinng in full force ever since. Man has taken over, and divine rule is no longer on Christ's shoulders. This is just as much a part of Babylon as any other sect or movement. It originated from the same source, is operated in the same way, and by the same spirit.

Brother Byrum saw it fall and it was wrecked beyond repair. Some preachers are staying in there trying to repair that old twisted, warped machine. Brother, it cannot be done. It is beyond repair. God has a system as old as the Church of God itself — a divinely organized machine, always new and workable, and needs no repair—why not use it?

This machine Brother Byrum saw is both political and commercial in its design and purpose. It furnishes offices to be sought, and salaries to be desired. This machine is not the true brand; it is of the Babylonian construction. It is being exposed by the Word of God. Twisted beyond repair, it will soon go down with the rest of Babylon to rise no more.

WHAT IS BABYLON?

Rev. 17:3-5—"So he carried me away in the spirit into the wilderness: and I saw a woman sit upon a scarlet colored beast, full of the names of blasphemy, having seven heads and ten horns.

"And the woman was arrayed in purple and scarlet colour, and decked with gold and precious stones and pearls, having a golden cup in her hand full of abominations and filthiness of her fornication:

"And upon her forehead was a name written, MYSTERY, BABYLON THE GREAT, THE MOTHER OF HARLOTS AND ABOMINATIONS OF THE EARTH."

(Rev. 18:1-4) "And after these things I saw another angel come down from heaven, having great power; and the earth was lightened with his glory.

"And he cried mightily with a strong voice, saying, Babylon the great is fallen, is fallen, and is become the habitation of devils, and the hold of every foul spirit, and a cage of every unclean and hateful bird.

"For all nations have drunk of the wine of the wrath of her fornication, and the kings of the earth have committed fornication with her, and the merchants of the earth are waxed rich through the abundance of her delicacies.

"And I heard another voice from heaven, saying, Come out of her, my people, that ye be not partakers of her sins, and that ye receive not of her plagues."

There has been much comment on the meaning of the word Babylon, as it appears in the Book of Revelation in the Bible. Rev. 14:8, and almost the entire chapters of

Rev. 17 and 18 are given to the subject of Babylon—what it is, what it does, and its consequences and final doom.

In dealing with the subject of Babylon, as given in the book of Revelation, we must remember that this is symbolic language. John wrote the book of the Revelation in 96 A.D., giving past, present, and future of the entire gospel day; but he wrote it in symbolic language, covering up its meaning until the time came when God was ready to reveal it. Webster says the definition of the word symbol is, "An emblem, or sign of something else; a type." So in looking for the real meaning of the word Babylon, as used in the book of Revelation we must look for something beside the original meaning of the word, which has reference to a city by that name.

The ancient City of Babylon was located on the banks of the Euphrates river. The history of its origination is not very clear. However, it dates back over two thousand years before Christ. It was the capital of Babylonia from the time of Hammurabi (2124 B.C.) to the end of the Chaldaean empire (539 B.C.). Most all classic writers have nothing to do with the ancient kingdom but deal altogether with the resuscitated and adorned residence of Nebuchadnezzar.

In the 11th chapter of Genesis we are given some history of the descendants of Noah who drifted into the land of Shinar and attempted to build a tower unto heaven. The people to this time were of one language, but God confused their language and their attempts to build were halted and they were scattered over the earth. Wherefore the tower was called Babel, or Confusion, from the Hebrew Balbel, "to confound". Babel is the Assyrian Babili, "the gate of God." Different conquerors tried to obliterate this tower, but its complete destruction was brought about by Nebuchadnezzar, whose reign began about 625 B. C.

Nebuchadnezzar built a great walled city, whose circumference was about 60 miles, located on both sides of the Euphrates River. This city was built square and much regularity was seen in the arrangements of its streets.

The west side seems to be the older part of the city, with the location of the ruins of the tower of Babel. In the center of the west side of this city stood the great heathen temple of Belus, or Baal. Also, on the west side of the river there seems to have been located the citadel of the ancient Babylonian Monarchy.

On the east side of the river stood the buildings of the Neo-Babylonian period, of which the Hanging Gardens are considered one of the seven wonders of the world.

About 606 B. C. Nebuchadnezzar, having gained many of the lost kingdoms, now restored Babylon as queen of the nations and began to build and restore the city of Babylon and many of the temples in the surrounding country. It was he who plundered the city of Jerusalem (606 B. C.) taking a host of the Israelites into Babylonian captivity. A few years later, he took the golden, sacred vessels of the temple, then tore it down, leaving it a heap of rubbish. This was a result of the children of Israel continually disobeying the commandments of God. They stayed in Babylonian captivity for seventy years, and then were permitted to return and rebuild the temple in Jerusalem. Israel was God's chosen people, and He had planned and provided that they should worship Him in His temple in the city of Jerusalem. For rebellion and disobedience they were captives in a strange land. "By the rivers of Babylon, there we sat down, yea, we wept, when we remembered Zion. We hanged our harps upon the willows in the midst thereof. For there they that carried us away captive required of us a song; and they that wasted us required of us mirth, saying, Sing us one of the songs of Zion. How shall we sing the Lord's song in a strange land?" Psa. 137:1-4. In the year 536 B.C. 42,300 Israelites were permitted to return and rebuild the temple in Jerusalem.

We are giving this sketch of history that it may be seen why the word Babylon is used as a symbol, or type in the book of Revelation. Let us notice some of the characteristics of the meaning of this word as derived from its original use.

We notice it had its origination with heathen people. It carried a meaning of confusion and bondage. It was a wicked, powerful nation, continually against God and His people, Israel. This word Babylon, as used by John in the book of Revelation, is intended to convey to us spiritual confusion, bondage, and wickedness in high places in the church. It is intended to show us the confused condition the church or professed religious people got into during the gospel day. It also shows us how people were brought under its power and bondage which was not of God. The background of this wicked and blasphemous city of Babylon is intended in type and symbol to convey to us the same wicked, sinful characteristics that exist in spiritual Babylon in the gospel day. The conditions that existed in the type is reflected in the anti-type of these symbols. So then in studying the nature of the type used in this symbol, we would expect to find spiritual confusion, bondage, and wickedness which are an abomination in the sight of God.

The old city Babylon was built by heathen nations of people who knew not the true worship of God. The new city of spiritual Babylon, as given in the Revelation, was built by a people who had lost the true standard of the Word and worship of God. So, then, in like manner, as literal Israel was carried into literal Babylon, we will find spiritual Israel, the church, carried into spiritual Babylon during the gospel day.

One of the first steps Israel made toward Babylonian bondage and confusion was when they rejected Samuel as their Judge, and wanted a king like other nations. Samuel lamented much about this, but God said to him, "They have not only rejected you but they have rejected Me." He further told them that their kings would become wicked, oppressive, and cruel. Their rebellion against God brought its final results of Babylonian captivity. After seventy years of Babylonian captivity they were permitted to return to their own land and rebuild the temple in Jerusalem.

Now, we want to notice some things that finally caused the church, in the gospel day, to become spiritual Babylon. History makes it clear that in the first candlestick age, of 270 years of the gospel day, God had a people who preached and practiced all of the Word of God. However, in the last of this age, many began to drift away from the true standard of truth. By 270 A. D. some began to turn from divine government in the church, by the Word and Spirit, and began to place this power and responsibility of government in the hands of men, who became wicked and oppressive. The people who held to the true Bible standard began to diminish in numbers, while the others increased. Within a few centuries the entire professed world was submerged into the wicked, cruel bondage of spiritual Babylon, (Catholicism). This wicked, cruel bondage continued until 1530 A. D. when Martin Luther and others began to expose some of its deceptions. This bondage and deception was, in part, broken. Many were made to see that people were made free from sin by repentance and faith in Jesus Christ, and not through the line of Popes, Bishops, and Priests.

These people were still in Babylonian bondage and confusion. They began to make an image to the beast of Catholicism. They left the Catholic church and began to make themselves churches of their own liking. Instead of letting Jesus be the head and governor of the church, they began to place the ruling power in the hands of men, many of whom became wicked and corrupt.

It seemed there was no end of sect and creed making during the 350 years of Protestant reign. There arose hundreds of churches, each one having his own doctrine, creed, and ritual; thus filling the religious world with confusion. Many of their practices and teachings contradicted the Bible and the teachings and practices of other creeds and sects. This division and confusion was, and still is, a stumbling block to the lost world. They wonder why the professed world do not speak the same thing as commanded by the Bible itself.

People in this kind of sect are not only confused but also in bondage. Its members are bound to its doctrines and ritual, many of which are contradictory to the plain Word of God. Yet, they must stand by its teachings and practices. This is bondage in spiritual Babylon. The souls of men crave freedom and the privilege to look into the Word of God for one's self; believe, live, and walk as he feels down deep in his own heart would please his Maker.

Spiritual Babylon is not only filled with confusion and bondage, but wickedness. It is wicked and sinful for one to contrive to change or disannul the Word of God and set up something of his own origin. In Matt. 16:18 Jesus said, "I will build my church." In Acts 2:47 we are told that "the Lord added to the church daily such as should be saved." This makes it clear that Jesus will take care of the building and the adding of members. He adds only those who are worthy. Man is sure to get the bad with the good. It is wicked to dishonor Christ as the head of the church. "He is the head of the body, the church." Col. 1:18. This plainly says that Jesus is the head of the church, that is the one He built. In Isa. 9:6 we read, "For unto us a child is born, unto us a son is given: and the government shall be upon his shoulder." Every honest and sincere soul does desire to let Jesus be the head and governor of His own church. It is wrong to change the seat of government from Christ to any man or group of men. To desire it is selfishness and coveteousness; to attempt it, is robbery.

Then, also, man-made organizations are filled with unsaved people. One may backslide, yet be a member in full fellowship and full authority, and equally privileged with the rest of the members.

Spiritual Babylon has a government by man. It is not divine because it is not of Christ, the head of the church. It is strictly of man's origination. They may pray, but it is certain that the Holy Spirit does not tell them that which may contradict the plain Word of God. It is blasphemy against Christ to claim He is directing and leading people to do contrary to His own teaching.

In Gen. 11:4 we have an account of the building of the tower of Babel. The purpose was as stated here to build a tower to reach heaven. In our enlightenment to-day it would seem foolish to undertake such a thing.

Many today in spiritual Babylon are making the same foolish endeavor. They are conforming to man-made teachings, doctrines, and requirements which promise to give them an abundant entrance into heaven at death. Nothing in the ritual of men can save a soul that is lost in sin. God will not accept even the most sincere devotions of worship and works of men. The blood of Jesus Christ is the only thing that will save a soul and make it a fit subject for heaven. This must be obtained separate from all ritualistic practices of men. If a soul gets saved it is because he repents of his sins and believes on the Lord Jesus for pardon, and not because of conforming to some teachings of men.

In attempting this spiritual tower to heaven in the gospel day, men have become confused and have fallen far short of heaven. It certainly is foolish to attempt such a structure, yet kings and captains in the realm of spiritual Babylon are attempting such a thing, and are so blind to spiritual things that they do not see the tower of spiritual Babylon is fallen, and God says, "Come out of her, my people." Rev. 18:4.

We notice another motive in Gen. 11:4, " . . . let us make us a name, lest we be scattered abroad. . ." This can surely be applied to all sects and movements. The leaders of such movements are called kings and captains in the book of Revelation, whose motive it is to make a name to hold them together. Each sect and movement, when dominated by man, always plan to hold its subjects so they will not be scattered. It is easy to see that the people in Babylon have the same spirit as those who attempted the tower of Babel.

There is no confusion in the Word of God when interpreted by the same Holy Spirit that inspired its writing. Truth does not confuse people. It is always error and deception that confuses. Where there is confusion, it is a sure sign some one has erred from the truth. God's truth is the only remedy for this world of confusion today. Bible unity is based on Bible truth; it cannot be had any other way.

The gospel day was divided into four periods of time relating to spiritual light and darkness. The morning church was ushered in with the full light of the gospel, which lasted until about 270 A.D. The dark day covered 1,260 years, from 270 to 1530 A.D. During this period of time Roman Catholicism darkened the earth with its gross deceptions. The cloudy day followed and covered the period of time from 1530 to 1880 A.D. After 1880 A.D. it is called the "Evening Time."

Through the inspiration of the Holy Spirit, the old Prophet Ezekiel saw the dark and cloudy day with its results. "For thus saith the Lord God; Behold, I, even I, will both search my sheep, and seek them out. As a shepherd seeketh out his flock in the day that he is among his sheep that are scattered; so will I seek out my sheep, and will deliver them out of all places where they have been scattered in the CLOUDY AND DARK DAY." Ezek. 34:11-12. "And it shall come to pass in that day (gospel), that the light shall not be clear nor dark: but it shall be one day which shall be known to the Lord, not day, nor night: but it shall come to pass, that at evening time it shall be light." Zech. 14:6-7.

Ezekiel tells us of a CLOUDY and a DARK DAY. Zechariah tells us of the cloudy day when it is not dark nor light, but at evening time it shall be light. The same gospel that made it light in the morning time makes it light in the evening time. The cloudy day ended in 1880 A.D. and since that time the same gospel of faith and practice that was preached in the morning of time is being preached and practiced in the evening of time.

In one of the above scriptures Ezekiel tells us that God's sheep were scattered during this cloudy and dark day; this means doctrinally and spiritually scattered and confused. In the dark day, Catholicism buried the nations in the darkness of its paganistic teachings. In the first part of the sixteenth century Bibles began to be scattered among the people, and the extreme darkness began to break with the small amount of light that started Protestantism through the "cloudy day." In this period of time the light was neither clear nor dark. The old devil and Satan working through the dragon powers brought in a flood of deception and a babel of confusion during the 350 years of Protestant sect and creed-making. Protestantism had light on how to obtain the new birth, and multitudes obtained this experience. Yet, much deception was introduced concerning these experiences, and many were engulfed in a babel of confusion. Remember this one thing, the correct understanding of Bible truth does not confuse. Error and deception always confuse the minds of people.

Many broke loose from the bondage and deceptions of Catholicism, and were led into a greater variety of deceptions in Protestantism. They left the original beast religion of Catholicism, made an image to it, which was Protestantism, and worshipped the image. You will find a description of the beast of Catholicism in Rev. 13:1-10. Then beginning with verse eleven, it deals with the two-horned beast which is Protestantism. I am giving this sketch of history to show WHAT BABYLON IS, AND WHERE IT ORIGINATED. The real meaning of BABY-

LON is CONFUSION. In the gospel day of antitype ful-fillment, it means spiritual CONFUSION.

The ancient city and domain of Babylon was heathen-istic in its religious worship, always in opposition to God and His way of worship. Spiritual Babylon, in the gospel day, reflects the same spirit of opposition to God and His truth, bringing people into deception and a Babel of con-fusion.

Babylon originated with men and always stands for CONFUSION. Even the master minds of great men do not run together in spiritual things. Only those who are led by the Holy Spirit can be led into the UNITY OF THE FAITH. SATAN is the author of division, but God is the author of UNITY AND TRUTH. Any time we leave the paths of leadership of the Spirit of God we im-mediately enter into the realm of BABYLONIAN CON-FUSION. Only the PURE in heart, who set their face to know Jesus Christ and His truth, by a "know so" reve-lation and witness of the Spirit, can be led into the UNITY OF THE FAITH OF THE GOSPEL. The Holy Spirit never leads contrary to the Word of God; they always agree.

The real meaning of the Word of God was lost sight of during the dark ages. God used a progressive method of bringing back his truth during the 350 years of Prot-estantism. He did not bring it all at once. He brought FIRST THINGS FIRST. Justification was preached for 200 years, then sanctification was preached as a second work of divine grace. This finished the great plan of redemp-tion from all sin, purifying the hearts of the people by faith.

God brought the truth of full and free salvation dur-ing the 350 years of Protestantism, but the enemy of all truth succeeded in getting men to teach beyond the leader-ship of the Spirit, introducing deceptions, doctrines, and traditions of men, leading men into a state of confusion and division. Groups could not work together. This left the religious world separated and divided into hundreds, yea, thousands of groups who could not work together. The word SECT means a formulated group, distinguished from others. This was so different to the plain teachings of the Word of God that the two witnesses, Word and Spirit, could not work as divine governor and leader. It was man-rule and not divine.

Now let us read Rev. 11:3 and 7-9, "And I will give power unto my two witnesses, and they shall prophesy a thousand two hundred and three score days, clothed in sackcloth." . . . "And when they shall have finished their testimony, the beast (Protestantism) that ascendeth out of the bottomless pit shall make war against them, and shall overcome them and kill them. And their dead bodies shall lie in the street of the great city (Babylon), which spiritually is called Sodom and Egypt, where also our Lord was crucified. And they of the people and kindreds and tongues and nations shall see their dead bodies three days and an half, and shall not suffer their dead bodies to be put in graves."

In verse 3 of this reading we are told how the Word and Spirit were covered up by the rubbish of Catholicism for 1,260 days, meaning years. They could not fill their place as governor and guide for those who got saved during this age of darkness. Then in verses 7-9 we are told of the two witnesses finishing their testimony in the 1,260 years of dark ages; then, in the next age that followed they were brought out in the open, or brought to the people again. Lying in the streets would signify that they were visible for all nations to see, during the 350 years, or three days and an half, of Protestant rule. They were said to be killed because they were not allowed to govern and guide the people who had gotten saved. Man-rule took the place of divine rule. The church is to be governed by the Spirit through its various gifts. You will find these enumerated in the 12th chapter of 1 Corinthians. God gives the right gift to each individual as He sees fit. These gifts furnish all that is needed for the church to be a live, working force, going forth conquering and to conquer. These gifts in operation in the church give sufficient power to save a sin-sick soul, the lost world and gives all power over the enemy, so that signs will follow according to the commission. The same God who calls, qualifies, and sends, also takes care of those whom He sends. "Go ye therefore, and teach all nations, baptizing them in the name of the Father, and of the Son, and of the Holy Ghost; teaching them to observe all things whatsoever I have commanded you: and, lo, I am with you alway, even unto the end of the world." Matt. 28:19-20. "And he said unto them, Go ye into all the world, and preach the gospel to every creature. He that believeth and is baptized shall be saved; but he that believeth not shall be damned. And these signs shall follow them that believe; in my name shall they cast out devils; they shall speak with new tongues; they shall take up serpents; and if they shall drink any deadly thing, it shall not hurt them; they shall lay hands on the sick, and they shall recover." Mark 16:15-18. This is all the organization the church needs. Power is promised for all the needs of both soul and body. For such a church, he has promised that signs will follow, showing God's recognition and power. A church that has the power God has promised, does not need man-made organizations. Any people who have adopted any creed or rules that are different from the above mentioned commission have departed from the faith of the gospel. God does not put his grace, power and victory on the preaching of deception. As long as men "send gifts one to another," the two witnesses will remain dead. Rev. 11:10.

Any kind of organization that man may set up is wrong, because it sets at naught the divine plan of God, and makes it of none effect. " . . . he (Jesus) is the head of the body, the church: who is the beginning, the first born from the dead; that in all things he might have the preeminence." Col. 1:18. When men are made the head of the church, Christ is robbed of His place. The headquarters of the Church that Jesus built, the Bible Church of God, is in heaven where the head of the church is located. That is where each member should go to get direction. "In all things he should have the preeminence." If we look to a man, or a group of men, they will become our headquarters, and may go wrong, but Jesus never gives the wrong command. All of the above apostate conditions are found in the Catholic and Protestant churches, and constitute BABYLON THE GREAT, THE MOTHER OF HARLOTS, AND ABOMINATIONS OF THE EARTH. Rev. 17:5.

The word Babylon, as used in the book of Revelation, has reference to the deceptions of Catholicism, Protestantism, and all so-called holiness movements. There is only one group excepted; that is the group "that follow the Lamb whithersoever he goeth." In Zach. 14:7 we are told, "That at evening time it shall be light." This evening light exposes all the deceptions of Babylon. All honest souls can hear, "Another voice, saying, COME OUT OF HER, MY PEOPLE." Rev. 18:4.

The "evening light," as spoken of by Zachariah, had its beginning following the cloudy day, which ended in 1880 A.D. The cloudy day brought some light, but not in its fullness. The "evening light" included the light that had been previously given in the cloudy day, and the full light and knowledge of the Divine Church of God, free from the deceptions of Babylon.

This evening light and truth was brought with the opening of the sixth seal, which began in 1880 A.D. "And I saw another angel (ministry of sixth seal) fly in the midst of heaven (heavenly places on earth), having the everlasting gospel to preach to them that dwell on the earth, and to every nation, and kindred, and tongue, and people;

"Saying with a loud voice, Fear God, and give glory to him; for the hour of his judgment is come: and worship him that made heaven and earth, and the sea, and the fountains of water. And there followed another angel (part of the sixth seal ministry), saying, Babylon is fallen, is fallen, that great city, because she made all nations drink of the wine of the wrath of her fornication. And the third angel followed them, saying with a loud voice, If any man worship the beast and his image (Babylon), and receive his mark in his forehead, or in his hand, the same shall drink of the wine of the wrath of God, which is poured out without mixture into the cup of his indigation; and he shall be tormented with fire and brimstone in the presence of the holy angels, and in the presence of the Lamb; and the smoke of their torment ascendeth up for ever and ever: and they have no rest day nor night, who worship the beast and his image, and whosoever receiveth the mark of his name." Rev. 14:6-11.

This scripture gives us an account of the beginning of the "evening light," and its results. This angel was the ministry of the sixth seal, and destined to go to all the world. This "everlasting gospel" was a full gospel. It confirmed the light and truth that was preached in the "cloudy day," and brought truth clarifying the complete plan of redemption, and a divine Church, the only one that Jesus built. This light that revealed a divine church exposed all Babylonian deceptions, and false churches of men.

A part of the message of this ministry was to tell people to "Fear God, and give glory to him, for the hour of his judgment is come." The Word of God should put a fear upon every soul. It seems there are many in whom "There is no fear of God before their eyes." Some do not seem to fear the judgment of God. Each truth, when disobeyed, has a penalty.

In verse 8 we are told of that part of the ministry who exposed Babylon, with its sins and judgments. This ministry said, "Babylon is fallen." This was given in the present tense. He means that it is not built on a scriptural foundation—the rock—but is built on the sand. He calls Babylon a "Great City." It is great because she hath made ALL NATIONS DRINK OF THE WINE OF THE WRATH OF HER FORNICATION. Babylonian confusion, with its deceptions, have gone everywhere; all nations have tasted it.

Romans 7:4 tells us that we should be married to Christ. The Church is to be the BRIDE, and JESUS IS THE GROOM. The bride is to obey the husband in all things. "Therefore as the church is subject unto Christ, so let the wives be to their own husbands in every thing." Eph. 5:24. We are to pledge our allegiance to Jesus Christ and Him only. "This is my beloved Son; hear ye him." When we turn and pledge our allegiance to doctrines and practices of men, or marry another while our first husband (Jesus) still lives, we COMMIT ADULTERY. This makes every individual that has joined or pledged their support to any part or portion of Babylon, a FORNICATOR. This is spiritual fornication. We are to worship God alone in spirit and in truth. Jesus hates spiritual fornication of His bride just as bad as He does literal fornication, and maybe worse.

In Rev. 21:8, John gives a summing up of the punishment of all classes that wilfully violate and do not keep the things written in this book. "But the fearful, and unbelieving, and the abominable, and murderers, and whoremongers, and sorcerers, and idolaters, and all liars, shall have their part in the lake which burneth with fire and brimstone: which is the second death." This lake of fire and brimstone is a symbol of the everlasting punishment of those who disobey God and refuse to keep His commandments.

In Rev. 14:11 it speaks of "the smoke of their torment." This smoke has reference to prayers. "And they have no rest day nor night," would set forth the fact that after people have heard God's message and still go on and worship the beast (Catholicism) and his image (Protestantism), they would have no more SOUL REST day nor night. Soul rest and peace of God leaves when people refuse to walk in the light.

Since this "evening light" started in 1880, God has had a people who stood true to the principles of a DIVINELY ORGANIZED and GOVERNED CHURCH. To do this, they had to stand against ALL BABYLONIAN

PRACTICES. Not every one that claimed to be in the Church of God stood true. There has been in every age hypocrites and imposters who claim to be the Church of God. Jesus had a Judas. But like Judas, they will not last long if the Holy Spirit fires are kept hot.

In Matt. 16:18, Jesus said, "I will build my church." In Acts 2:47, "And the Lord added to the church daily such as should be saved." The Lord did the saving and the adding to the church. Jesus built, or organized, his church on the day of Pentecost through the operation of the Holy Ghost. Through the giving of spiritual gifts to different individuals, "severally as he wills," the church started its divine operation. Each individual sought God to know their place and how and when to fill it. It is true that OUR GIFTS WILL MAKE A PLACE FOR US IN GOD'S CHURCH. There is no friction or mix-up when all are led by the Holy Spirit. It is said that the church at Antioch, about 100 years after Christ, numbered 100,000 saints. God can govern 100,000 just as easy as he can one dozen. Regardless of numbers, God can pick His man and make His will known. We are not told just how to do it, only to seek His face until His will is known. This was the practice of the early church until the apostasy set in, and man-rule took over. The early church had no earthly headquarters or place from which to receive advice, instructions, or orders. No boards or committees were appointed to take care of spiritual things. Questions were not settled by a majority vote. They honored Jesus Christ and the Holy Spirit as their head and governor. The church operated through the gifts of the Spirit with power, and signs following. The sick were healed in both soul and body, devils were cast out, and signs followed insomuch that no man durst join himself to them. This is what it took to make a divine church in the morning time. We lost it in the "dark and cloudy day." "At evening time it shall be light." The evening light, which came in 1880, with the opening of the sixth seal, revealed the same kind of a church with the same kind of spiritual government. D. S. Warner and many others in the sixth seal taught and practiced this kind of church government. The evening light of the gospel is the same as the morning light. The same truth preached and practiced in the evening time will produce the same results as the morning time. God had a church that trusted him for all things through the sixth seal, which ended 1930 A.D.

The same light that brought the church back to the Bible standard of truth, exposed the deceptions of Babylon, with its unscriptural doctrines and practices. As the call went forth, many of God's people came out of Babylonian confusion, and took their stand for a divine church. Those who saw the light and refused to walk in it, lost their souls and went into darkness, with the Sun of Righteousness becoming as black as sackcloth of hair. Many fought the truth, making all kinds of excuses, hiding in the holes and rocks of Babylon, with the light having gone out in their souls.

The two witnesses, the Word and Spirit, having now "stood upon their feet," tormented the people of fallen Babylon. So they started to substitute UNION for the UNITY of God's people. This developed into the World Council of Churches, which is described in Rev. 17 as—"BABYLON THE GREAT, THE MOTHER OF HARLOTS."

During the fifty year period of the sixth seal, this glorious gospel that made clear a divine church, free from Babylonian practices, reached some of the Babylonian world. It seems clear that it did not reach all of it, for only a "Tenth part of the city (Babylon) fell." Rev. 11:13. When he said, "Babylon is fallen," it seems clear that John meant that the unscriptural foundation on which it is built is exposed and its fallen condition is made clear. It is like the house that was built upon the sand. There are many, perhaps some honest people, who have built their spiritual house upon the sand, only to have it fall through the storms and fires of the "evening light." There were a few, in comparison, who stood against much opposition and persecution, who had a table set in the presence of their enemies, and ate the good things as a result of walking in the evening light. "And the same hour was there a great earthquake, and the tenth part of the city (Babylon) fell, and in the earthquake were slain of men seven thousand: and the remnant were affrighted, and gave glory to the God of heaven." Rev. 11:13.

This seven thousand represents a great number who would not walk in the light, and were spiritually slain by the sword of the Spirit of light. Only a few were affrighted, accepted the truth and gave God glory. Those refusing, lost out with God, but kept their profession. They loved something else more than they loved the light and truth that was preached to them. " . . . because they received not the love for the truth, that they might be saved. And for this cause God shall send them strong delusion, that they should believe a lie: that they all might be damned who believed not the truth, but had pleasure in unrighteousness." 2 Thess. 2:10-12. It is a terrible condition for a person to get under a delusion; they lose their salvation and acceptance with God, yet do not realize it. They may preach, pray, sing, raise the budget, gather the numbers into their ranks, yet be DEAD and do not know it. No doubt the number represented by the "seven thousand" went on with their Babylonian profession, thinking they were right, because here and there a soul seemed to be blessed.

It was those who did not walk in the light when it came, that lost out with God. There were many who never had a chance to hear the truth concerning the Divine Church of God, or to see the sins of Babylon. If they were born again and lived to all the light they had, there would not be any question about their acceptance with God. "But if we walk in the light as he (Christ) is in the light, we have fellowship one with another, and the blood of Jesus Christ his Son cleanseth us from all sin." 1 John 1:7. Some have lost their fellowship with Christ and His people, and all they have left is a Babylonian fellowship with some group or sect.

I want us to notice the combat, in the sixth seal, between those who had accepted the truth and those who refused it. There was a battle between these two forces. There was a great number who stood like a rock in the billows. They lived on their knees, with a decision to walk in the light as it came. Many became seed among the thorns and thistles, and on the stony ground, swapped the truth for a delusion, only to wake up at the judgment, and find out that they had sold their souls for naught.

The truth of God's Word will bring a division between those that love God and His truth and those that love something else better. The one great purpose of the gospel is SEPARATION. It separates right from wrong, the good from the bad. "Suppose ye that I am come to give peace on earth? I tell you, Nay; but rather division." Luke 12:51. Babylon had within its rank every kind, both good and bad. This evening light brought a separation. Once more God has a people free from Babylonian practices, standing on Mt. Zion, the fullness of "evening light" truth, free from the bondage of Babylonian practices and man-rule.

Toward the last of the sixth seal the enemy of UNITY AND TRUTH succeeded in dividing the saints of God on technicalities of untruth. Some tried to impose certain standards and customs of their own thinking upon all the church. Many good saints submitted to this for the sake of unity and harmony. Being the seed of fanaticism, it soon made itself mandatory and binding on others, and like all divisional and unscriptural spirits, it broke fellowship with those who would not conform to their customs. Fanaticism goes beyond the true meaning of modesty. I believe every spirit filled saint of God will have a true sense of modesty. Babes in Christ, and some of those less spiritual ones, may need some reproof, but not to the forming of certain styles and customs which the Bible does not make clear.

Some of the good saints saw the extent of bondage this was leading to, broke with its man-imposed customs, and declared their freedom again. It is always right to declare ourselves free from anything that is wrong. We may be misunderstood, BUT TRUTH COVERED UP WILL RISE AGAIN, and those that accept it will rise with it.

Many of those who took their stand against the imposed customs of men were still blessed with power and victory with signs following. There were a few who, with unprejudiced minds, got on their knees and prayed through to heaven and got an answer, which is always Biblical, sane, and sound. God is interested in the heart being made pure, clean, and free from the "lust of the flesh, lust of the eye, and the pride of life." God looketh not upon the outward appearance, but upon the heart. Man looketh upon the outward appearance. Sin in the heart may show through some outward performance, but outward performance is not always a sure indication that there is sin in the heart.

This divisional spirit caused many on BOTH SIDES to lose out with God. This became the devil's tool. Some got discouraged and gave up, while some on both sides got under a bad spirit and became critically bitter and harsh toward those that did not see as they saw things. This did not only cause a break of fellowship between brethren, but led to a break of fellowship between many and God. No one can become critical, harsh, and hold grudges and still prosper in his soul. I came through this without being affected with the unscriptural traditions of either side. I was in the mountains preaching the gospel to lost souls. I thank God for those years of isolation. Tradition is hard to break, but I find many honest saints of God who want freedom from the tradition of the customs of men, and are willing to give the same freedom to their brethren. God is once more uniting His people on the TRUE PRINCIPLES of the gospel, and not traditional customs of men. Here is a little rule given unto me which I wish you would consider well. "ANY TIME WE STANDARDIZE CUSTOMS WE GET OURSELVES AND OTHERS INTO TROUBLE."

There are some people who do not wear a necktie, and do not have any kind of a musical instrument in the church, and God blesses them. We only have to look around to find congregations of the same customs and practices who are spiritually dead. Then, it is an undeniable fact that some who wear a necktie and have a piano or organ in the church are blessed with the presence and power of God. There are others, with like customs, who are twice dead, plucked up by the roots. Since in many things, God does not care IF WE DO, OR WE DON'T. They are left to our sanctified judgment, and should never be quibbled about. Why make ourselves a part of Babylon because SOME ONE ELSE DOES OR DOESN'T? God certainly will take notice if we get malice in our hearts about these things, for HE LOOKS UPON THE HEART. Prov. 6:16-17. One of the seven things God hates is a "proud look." Pride in the heart is sin, and usually shows itself on the outside. Some are proud because they do certain things, others are proud because they don't do them.

Now, I have tried to find the central line of truth. It would be easy to slip to either side and find plenty of technicalities to argue about. This I refuse to do, for that is what has caused the trouble in the past. Amen.

It does not make people spiritual to bind upon them commandments and customs of men to keep them from worldly things; neither does religious freedom make folks spiritual who love to follow the world. A truly redeemed soul will certainly strive with all his heart to do the WILL of the REDEEMER, and will crave with all his heart to keep himself unspotted from the world. He will want to dress, walk, and talk so as to influence the most people possible to accept the salvation of the Lord Jesus. The Word of God grants this kind of freedom to every blood-washed saint.

By the end of the sixth seal, 1930, that spiritual disease of lukewarmness had begun to fix its grip on the religious world. This killed spiritual zeal, courage, and a

passion for lost souls, causing a loss of power and leadership of the spirit. This caused all religious movements that
had any spiritual light to lose their power with God. This
opened the door for COMPROMISE, DECEPTIONS, and
WORLDLINESS to be brought into the church. God's
action against "lukewarmness" was a spewing out of his
mouth. This left the people without divine leadership to
act under man-rule. Back to Babylonian practices was the
ONLY open door. For awhile, the most spiritual directed
the church under divine leadership, but soon the government of the church was changed into a democracy with a
majority vote ruling. Jesus as head and governor of the
church was out. Man with his Babylonian practices stepped
in and took over. Organization by man, that was at one
time so strongly preached against as an enemy of divine
government, swept through congregations, camp meetings,
and assemblies. Boards, committees, and high officers
were elected or appointed to direct the procedure of the
church. The National assemblies took preeminence over
all the rest, making it a headquarters. This took place in
many holiness movements, who, at one time, did not believe
in such organizations. These high offices, with popularity
and salaries, offered an open door for the gratification of
the flesh, FROM WHICH NO HUMAN ORGANIZA-
TION CAN BE KEPT FREE.

Many movements, that at one time had a passion for
lost souls, have streamlined their program with a great
Money Raising campaign. It would be a good time to remember that scripture where it says, "The LOVE of money
is the root of all evil." Local congregations get their ser-
mons and thoughts weeks, and sometimes months, ahead
from headquarters.

Men are picked to fill the pulpit on certain occasions
if they are in sympathy with the things being done. The
underhanded IRON hand of ecclesiastical rule plans its
program and picks its men. The means of coersion is boy-
cotting. God knew that such assemblies would soon become a crafty, degraded, lustful, ecclesiastical hierarchy.

This all belongs over in the realm of Babylon. Any church ceases to be the Church of God when Jesus ceases to be the head.

Not only has divine government been supplanted by man-rule, but worldliness has followed as one of the effects of lukewarmness. When Christ went out, the spirit of the world came in. Many lost their sense of modesty and plainness of apparel. Decorations began to appear on the outside that showed what was on the inside. Many began to look for excuses to go back to ornamentation that at one time they felt was out of place. Many attend unwholesome places of amusement. The preacher does not preach against them any more; in fact, many of them attend themselves..

As a consequence of the above mentioned things, FAITH IS GONE. Lukewarmness has sprayed its deadly effect upon Faith. Dead faith does not have the signs following it. The preachers, instead of preaching FAITH in the GREAT PHYSICIAN, recommend earthly physicians. The oil vial that at one time was found in the pocket of the preacher, is changed to the vile prescribed by the physician. The ministry that used to stir up the devil by the preaching of the pure Word of God and then through faith in God, cast them out, does not even disturb them any more. With many preachers the gifts of miracles, faith, and healing are superseded by modern discoveries of men. With many, HEAVENLY WISDOM is laid on the shelf while Wisdom of the World is streamlined. The real gift of preaching is not the elecutionary art of the oratory of men. All the anointing many preachers have today is the anointing of a criminal lawyer who, by HIS OWN POWER, tries to win his case.

Lukewarmness opens the d o o r f o r BABYLONIAN deceptions and practices. When people are spewed out, God, Jesus, and the Holy Spirit steps back and leaves them on their own. The only alternative for such people is to accept Babylonian practices. The greatest tragedy of all is that they are "destitute, miserable, blind, and naked," and do not know it. Dead people cannot produce Holy Spirit fire and, as a consequence, this lukewarm age has become a ripe field and an open door for the devil's WILD FIRE.

Babylon has introduced men's names to identify certain groups and movements. Jesus prayed for his people to be kept in His Father's name. In the Epistles we find the apostles addressed them to the Church of God. In twelve places we find the saints addressed as the Church of God. Regardless of where they were located, this was the name given them. Many church groups are named after their founder, or in harmony and memory of some particular doctrine that characterize that particular movement. This is some more of the CONFUSION OF BABYLON THE GREAT, THE MOTHER OF HARLOTS. She mothers her daughters of confusion. Mother Babylon has some of her daughters marked with some political move, such as the north or south, having been affected by the slavery question.

It takes more than the name to make the Bible Church of God. It takes FAITH, EXPERIENCE, and PRACTICE.

Our FAITH must be based on the right interpretation of the Word of God. The Holy Spirit only gives ONE interpretation. There are many wrong interpretations, but there is only one that is right. Only those that seek with all their hearts and with a pure and unselfish motive will find God's way. Sincerity is not enough. We must have the Holy Ghost, whom Jesus said would guide us into all truth, dwelling in our hearts. The right interpretation ALWAYS harmonizes with HOLINESS AND UNITY OF FAITH AND PRACTICE, as laid down in the New Testament Word of God. Anything that breeds CONTENTION AND DIVISION CONTRARY TO THE TRUE TEACHINGS OF THE WORD OF GOD, IS OF BABYLON. The true Word of God ALWAYS causes division. This kind of division is right. God is pleased with it. It separates from all that displeases God, and He is the one that we must seek to please. The work of the Word and Spirit in our hearts starts with the principles of division—separating us from sin and the world. As true knowledge of the Word of God increases it separates us from Babylonian deceptions. Those who love things in Babylon become the ENEMIES of those who love and accept the true way of Jesus. "Think not that I am come to send peace on the earth: I came not to send peace, but a sword. For I am come to set a man at variance against his father, and the daughter against her mother, and the daughter-in-law against her mother-in-law. And a man's foes shall be they of his own household." Matt. 10:34-36. The Bible must ALWAYS be interpreted to harmonize with the above scriptures. God wants his church UNIFIED according to the teachings of Bible unity, and separated from, and against ALL Babylonian practices and teachings. God has a people who have heard enough gospel to get saved, but in many ways are in darkness. They are not "saints in light." They are in Babylonian confusion. God, in this "evening time," is offering LIGHT and is demanding His people to come out. Rev. 18:4. God's people as a family are in all stages of development. It seems that some will never grow up. Many have not reached the place in ENLIGHTENMENT called "Mount Sion," God's Mountain of Truth. They are still in the hills of Babylon and confusion.

At this time of "evening light" God is gathering His people back to the Mt. Sion standards taught in the morning church. "And I looked, and, lo, a Lamb stood on the Mount Sion, and with him an hundred forty and four thousand, having his Father's name written in their foreheads." Rev. 14:1. John saw a symbol of a great host, symbolized by "an hundred forty and four thousand," standing upon God's mountain of truth. Light, that had revealed the true Bible Church of God, had been preached, beginning in the sixth seal, 1880. Those who walked in the light had reached the top of Mount Sion. They had their

Father's name written in their forehead, instead of "Mystery Babylon." Saints who walk in the light retain their salvation, and ascend Mount Sion, and those that refuse to walk in the light, lose their salvation, and stay in the hills of Babylon.

Salvation is always essential to being a member of God's church, but you may be a member in good standing of some Babylonian church, and not be saved at all. One great outstanding difference is that "God sets the members in the body (the church) as it pleases him," (1 Cor. 12:18) and man does all the setting in Babylonian groups. Two contrasting results are, God keeps His church pure and clean, and man can't do this.

The kings and captains of Babylon in this evening light of the the sixth and seventh seals are "tormented" by its message of Bible truth that exposes the SINS AND DI-VISIONS of BABYLON. Instead of accepting UNITY on the terms of the Bible, they are substituting UNION of all their unscriptural creeds. There is a great move by the leaders of spiritual Babylon to UNITE all creeds and religious movements, developing into a gerat WORLD COUNCIL OF CHURCHES. The uniting of all unscriptural sects cannot make the BIBLE CHURCH OF GOD. Neither will it eliminate her sins. The uniting of unscriptural, unholy movements c a n never produce a H O L Y church. Unscriptural faiths and practices, when united, are still heretical. There is just one way to have a Bible church, and that is to COME OUT OF BABYLON and take the TRUE WORD AND SPIRIT FOR OUR GUIDE. God will guide the honest seeker, who is without a selfish motive.

We are now living in the last part, or closing of the "evening light" dispensation. The seventeenth chapter of the book of Revelation gives us a present description of MODERN BABYLON, as she is and operates at the present time.

In this chapter we have an adulterous woman, sitting on a scarlet colored beast, full of names of blasphemy.

Beast religion is FALSE CHRISTIANITY. The woman is the WOULD-BE bride of Christ—the FALSE BRIDE. This false bride is riding the Beast of false religion. Beast religion has lifted up its head in opposition to Christ, "the Head of the Church," in each of the seven candlestick ages of the entire gospel day. These ten horns represent the devil working in paganism from the time of the Babylonian Empire, in Daniel's time, on to the end of the gospel day. These beasts that represent Babylonian religions are pagan in their origination. This beast is red, the color of the dragon. (Red means death.) The dragon had "given him his seat, and power and great authority." Rev. 13:1-10. This 17th chapter beast is the unionizing in the Council of Churches, the results of Babylon in the entire gospel day. We are told in verse 11, "Even he is the eight, and is of the seven." The spirit of UNION in Babylon is forming this EIGHTH BEAST, yet he is of the same spirit that has dominated in Babylon in the entire seven ages. (For greater light on this subject, get our latest book, "REVELATION, WITH GOSPEL AND PROPHECY.")

This "evening light" has made it clear that JESUS JUST HAS ONE BRIDE, ONE CHURCH. Now the enemy of all truth is endeavoring to UNITE all his deceptions into ONE BRIDE, through the World Council of Churches. This woman, in this 17th chapter, shows us her moral status.

In verse 3, John was carried down into the "wilderness" of Babylonian confusion to see this woman. She will always be found there. She was arrayed in king's apparel, purple and scarlet. She was decked with gold and precious stones and pearls. These are used to represent the Word of God. All deceptive religions have some of the Word of God to cover their deceptions. This woman has much truth hanging on her, yet inwardly she is a HARLOT. What she has to offer is in a GOLDEN CUP, "full of abominations and filthiness of her fornication." This has reference to SPIRITUAL things. When people pledge their allegiance to harlot churches of men, they become

SPIRITUAL FORNICATORS. With many, God has winked at ignorance in the past, but now in this "evening light" he commandeth, "Come out of her, my people."

"And upon her forehead was a name written, MYSTERY BABYLON THE GREAT, THE MOTHER OF HARLOTS AND ABOMINATIONS OF THE EARTH." This woman has "Mystery Babylon" written in her forehead where everybody can see it. This great Council of Churches is full of mysterious CONFUSION. Any fair-minded person can see the confusion of uniting all the different sects, creeds, and churches into one great Federation. "Mystery Babylon the Great" certainly would be the right name. It is further stated that she is the "MOTHER OF HARLOTS." Her children are just like their mother; they are spiritual fornicators. They are untrue to Christ, the Head of the Church. They have turned and married another— this is adultery. All who are a part of this false bride are spiritual HARLOTS.

In verse 6, John saw the woman "Drunk with the blood of the saints, and with the blood of the martyrs of Jesus." This harlot woman has led even saints into her deceptions, causing them to backslide, give up, and die spiritually. She also has caused many to live such ungodly lives that they crucified the Lord afresh and put him to an open shame. Her fornication has caused the spiritual death of many of God's people; she is guilty of their blood.

After John had seen this woman sitting on this scarlet colored beast, he marveled, because he did not understand what it meant. In verse 7, "And the angel said unto me, I will tell thee the mystery of the woman, and the beast that carried her, which had seven heads and ten horns." This beast had seven heads, one in each of the seven candlestick ages, in opposition to Christ, the Head of the Church. Rev. 17:8, "The beast that thou sawest was, and is not; and shall ascend out of the bottomless pit (heathenism), and go into perdition: and they that dwell on the earth shall wonder, whose names were not written in the book of life from the foundation of the world, when they behold the beast that was, and is not, and yet is." This beast, before the dark and cloudy day, "WAS" a world power. After 1880 A.D., this power was broken, and he "is not" a world power. "And yet is" a world power in the seventh seal age. This "Eighth Beast," the Council of Churches, is influencing many nations today, and is fast becoming a world power again. It seems the entire religious world is "wandering after the beast"; going into, and cooperating with it. The great majority of people who are supporting the Council of Churches are dead spiritually. Their names are not written in the Lamb's Book of Life. Those who are saved and on fire for God, and walking in the light, will not support the "Eighth beast" powers. In this seventh seal age the devil has succeeded in spraying the germs of that fatal disease, "lukewarmness," into the spiritual veins of the church; as a result, many have become lukewarm and spewed out, AND ARE A PREY FOR THE EIGHTH BEAST POWERS. Even the Church of God movement, those that had victory and power and preached against such things in the sixth seal, are now cooperating with the Council of Churches. Many have compromised and let down, yet God still has a people, a remnant, who are still standing on "The Mount Sion," holding the Bible standards of the Church of God HIGH above the hills of Babylon.

In verse 9, the seven mountains are false teaching in the seven ages of the gospel day, in opposition to the Mount Sion of the Bible. The woman was carried through each age on these mountains of deception. The seven kings has reference to the deceptive ruling power of the seven ages. Five of them fell, or went down, at the beginning of the sixth seal; the other was in existence through the sixth seal. The other one came in the seventh seal and lasted only a short time. "This beast that was, and is not, even he is the eighth, and is of the seventh, and goeth into perdition."

. The uniting of the Council of Churches today, the eighth beast, is the working of the same spirit that has worked in all the beasts before it. It always opposed God and TRUTH, and will oppose it until it goes into perdition at the end. The working of this seventh king, or eighth beast powers, are against God's way. It is wicked and abominable, with blasphemy against God. It is the same old spirit that "opened his mouth in blasphemy against God, to blaspheme his name, and his tabernacle (church), and them that dwell in heaven (the church)." Rev. 13:6.

In this eighth beast they advocate that ALL RELIGIONS ARE GOOD, and should unite their efforts to get people everywhere to join THE ONE OF THEIR CHOICE. All must have the spirit of TOLERATION in order to work with those who hold, practice, and teach things they do not believe. In ord: to work with this beast power it is necessary to qu.t preaching doctrine. The WEAKER the message the better it fits. Many of the leaders in the eighth beast are skeptics, evolutionists, infidels, and even some are Communists. The true people of God have no FELLOWSHIP with such people as these, and God says, "Come out from among them, and be separate." It is easy to see that the eighth beast is a combination of all the deceptions in the past, and is against the TRUTH that promotes and builds the REAL CHURCH OF GOD. The devil is succeeding in getting many to settle down and be at peace with sin and deception; calmly ride this beast of UNION, streamlined with all this MODERNISTIC FAITH KILLING, AND TRUTH ANNULING, PROGRAMIZING IN THE REALM OF HUMAN WISDOM. This beast is being refueled and throttled by a lukewarm, spewed out, carnal, coveteous, heretical hierarchy. All this is in opposition to DIVINE GOVERNMENT by the WORD AND SPIRIT OF GOD. Jesus will never be the head of the church with such teaching and practice. And when people get light and understanding, and see this abomination, yet REFUSE to walk in the light, they DIE SPIRITUALLY and lose their souls. They may still be a part of BABYLON THE GREAT, operate seminaries, send missionaries, raise a large budget, and put over a great program, yet be dead, powerless, and without God.

I would like to quote from a book written by Dr. George Herbert Betts, professor of Religious Education at Northwestern University, a Methodist school in Evanston, Ill. The book is entitled, "The Belief of Seven Hundred Ministers" and is published by the Abbington Press of the M. E. Church. This is the belief of seven hundred ministers in twenty different denominations in our country concerning different Bible subjects. Following are a few of the high points:

They all believe there is a God; that He exists.

80% believe in the Trinity: God, the Son and the Holy Ghost.

87% believe God is all powerful.

60% believe in a devil.

55% believe in an inspired Bible.

71% had accepted the new birth—regeneration.

70% accepted Christ's atonement.

57% believe heaven is a prepared place.

72% believe in man's resurrection.

66% believe that Christ will judge all.

33% denied that Christ ever performed a miracle.

18% of the young ministers believe Adam fell.

60% of the older ministers believe there is a devil, against 9% of the younger ministers.

55% of the older ministers believe the Bible was inspired against 8% of the younger.

84% of the older ministers believe in Christ's resurrection; only 42% of the younger believe this doctrine.

25% of the younger ministers believe Christ was born of a virgin, conceived by the Holy Ghost.

The two hundred young ministers were seminary students. This shows us what seminaries are doing for simple

FAITH in the Word of God. If the above figures are anywhere near a fair test, the condition is terrible and getting worse. Many who have "Church of God" over the church house door on the outside have Babylon practices on the inside. In order for saints to gather on God's Mt. Sion of TRUTH, they must leave the HILLS OF BABYLON practices.

In Rev. 17:12-14, John tells us about the horns of this eighth beast. These are the same in number as the ten horns on the dragon of Rev. the 12th chapter, and the same as the fourth beast of Daniel the 7th chapter. These are referring to the spirit of paganism from Daniel's time to the end of the gospel day. These ten horns represent all the pagan spirits and wild fire powers at work in the eighth beast, pretending to be the powers of the Holy Ghost. Much of the noise, demonstrations, and power seen in many of these so-called Holy Ghost and healing campaigns are of the devil, the ruler of the eighth beast powers. We only have to look closely into the Word of God to see its working does not harmonize with the plain teachings of the Bible. The devil is holding up before the people this unionized, World Council of Churches as the BRIDE OF CHRIST. He is clothing her with this false power of signs and wonders for the purpose of deceiving those who are looking for demonstrations. The original movements of the beast are dead spiritually. "Having a form of godliness, but denying the power thereof." The ten horns represent all these HOLINESS MOVEMENTS springing up in this present age. They are of the eighth beast, because they are of the DRAGON SPIRIT. With their wildfire power, they burn and scorch the rest of these dead, formal, lifeless movements, and, as it were, "Eat her flesh, and burn her with fire."

These horns are represented as kings. It is said they will make war with the Lamb. The "One mind" they have is TO FIGHT TRUTH. They are all set in that direction. It is said, "They have received no kingdom as yet." This great mass of eighth beast powers, heading the COUNCIL OF CHURCHES, believe in a MILLENNIUM, and that in the millennium, THEY WILL POSSESS A KINGDOM. The millennium theory has swept Babylon with all its falsified fancies of a FUTURE LITERAL KINGDOM. Jesus said, "My kingdom is not of this world." John 18:36. When He comes, it is not to SET UP A KINGDOM, but to "DELIVER UP THE KINGDOM TO THE FATHER," the one He set up at His first coming. 1 Cor. 15:24. "But the day of the Lord will come as a thief in the night; in the which the heavens shall pass away with a great noise, and the elements shall melt with fervent heat, the earth also and the works that are therein shall be BURNED UP." II Peter 3:10. When this earth is burned up, there is no place for a millennium with an EARTHLY kingdom. "Behold, I shew you a mystery; we shall not all sleep, but we shall all be changed, in a moment, in the twinkling of an eye, at the last trump: for the trumpet shall sound, and the dead shall be raised incorruptible, and we shall be changed. For this corruptible must put on incorruption, and this mortal must put on immortality." I Cor. 15:51-53. This takes place at the second coming of Christ. Immortal beings will have no need of raising corn and wheat, or anything that pertains to an EARTHLY kingdom. In John 14:2-3, Jesus says, "I go to prepare a place for you. And if I go and prepare a place for you, I will come again and receive you unto myself; that where I am there YE may be also." Jesus will have that place prepared to receive HIS BRIDE, THE CHURCH, at His second coming. The judgment and separating the sheep from the goats will be a quick work. "Then we which are alive and remain (the living) shall be caught up together with them (those that have died) in the clouds, and meet the Lord in the air;

and so shall we ever be with the Lord" in the place He has prepared for His bride.

There will be no millennium for the wicked. They will be judged and separated from the righteous at His appearing. There will be no need or place for a millennium after the wicked have heard that sad command, "Depart from me, ye cursed, into EVERLASTING FIRE prepared for the devil and his angels." Matt. 25:41. Some teach that the wicked will have another chance to get saved after the return of Christ. This is another one of the devil's deceptions to soothe the condemned conscience and make them believe they will have another chance in the millennium or some future age, after the second coming of Christ. All these fancied deceptions belong down in Babylon, and God said, "Come out of her, MY PEOPLE." Brother, if you are one of the Lord's sheep, it is time to get out of Babylon. It is not safe to stay in a thing that is FALLEN.

At the present time the devil is filling these eighth beast powers of BABYLON THE GREAT with wicked men and wickedness of all kinds. "This know also, that in the last days perilous times shall come. For men shall be lovers of their own selves, coveteous, boasters, proud, blasphemers, disobedient to parents, unthankful, unholy, without natural affections, truce breakers, false accusers, incontinent, fierce, despisers of those that are good, traitors, heady, highminded, lovers of pleasure more than lovers of God; having a form of godliness, but denying the power thereof: FROM SUCH TURN AWAY. . . (verse 7); ever learning, and NEVER able to come to the knowledge of the truth. As Jannes and Jambres withstood Moses, so do these also resist the truth; men of corrupt minds, reprobate concerning their faith." II Tim. 3:1-8.

Most all people believe that we are living in the "last days." If we are, we surely ought to be able to see the things mentioned in the above scripture. If we SEE THEM, surely we are living "in the last days." All we have to do is to open our eyes and look, for the fulfillment is NOW. Anywhere you find Babylon, you will find the above mentioned things, and anywhere you find these things, it WILL BE BABYLON. Anywhere you find organizations set up, and run by men, you will find the above mentioned things. God ONLY can build a HOLY CHURCH and keep it holy. We are living in a great age of EDUCATION, but people are not coming to the knowledge of the TRUTH. Many have resisted the truth until they have BECOME TRUTH FIGHTERS. "Multitudes in the valley of decision," and because they did not wish to retain a love for the TRUTH, "God shall send them strong delusion, that they should believe a lie; that they all may be damned who believed not the truth." II Thess. 2:10-12. Those that do not love the TRUTH enough to accept it and live it, WILL SOON FIND PLEASURE IN UNRIGHTEOUSNESS, and FIGHT THE TRUTH.

All may know the truth if they will. Those who are lovers of their own selves, boasters, heady, high-minded, will never accept the truth. None of those described in II Tim. 3:1 will have the truth when they hear it. Even in this age of perilous times, God still has a people WHO ARE WALKING IN ALL THE LIGHT THEY HAVE. Those who are accepting the fullness of the present light are WALKING out of Babylon into this marvelous freedom of God's glorious Mt. Sion Church. God gathered out in the sixth seal 144,000 on Mt. Sion. This is a symbol of a great number of people brought back to the TRUE standards according to God's mountain of truth. This great number were said to be standing with the Lamb on Mt. Sion, harping with their harps. They were harping HOLINESS, UNITY IN THE TRUTH, A DIVINE CHURCH, AND BABYLON IS FALLEN, and COME OUT OF

HER, MY PEOPLE. They were not defiled with women—man churches. There was no guile in their mouths. This message was plain, simple and understandable. Many saw it, but only a few rid themselves of selfish motives and accepted it. Few in comparison, yet a great host of true saints did accept it and became the Mt. Sion Church of God. Nearing the close of the sixth seal age, compromise through lukewarmness broke in and the majority of this great host ceased to continue to be the Mt. Sion Church of God.

In this seventh seal age many are being stirred and moved back to the Bible standard again. "The watchman shall lift the voice, with the voice together shall they sing: for they shall see eye to eye WHEN THE LORD SHALL BRING AGAIN SION." God brought it once in the sixth seal, and He is bringing it again, the second time, in the seventh seal age.

Once more God has a people coming out of every phase of Babylon accepting a full salvation, a divine church, and welcoming the Holy Spirit with all His gifts and power and governmental authority. God has a people who see EYE TO EYE. All who see Sion, SEE IT ALIKE. If we do not see alike, some one DOES NOT SEE SION. In Heb. 12:22, Paul says, "But ye are come unto Mount Sion." You cannot be in Sion and Babylon at the same time. It takes obedience to the true Bible standards of truth to be in Sion. Without this, everyone will find himself in Babylon.

This fulness of Bible light brought to us in this present age is called "The camp of the saints." In many places in the Word of God his people are spoken of as walking, running, or in some kind of travel in a forward march. In the "Camp of the saints," a stopping is signified. Once more the fullness of truth is being brought to us. We are commanded to camp on the truth, and never leave it. "Let no man steal your crown." Prophecy, gospel, and the Revelation all teach we are living in the last age. The end of time is not far hence. We are seeing "The fig tree putting forth her tender branches." Once more Jesus is bringing again Sion. A few are taking their stand for truth, stopping, and remaining in the "Camp of the Saints." Many have started, and because of opposition and persecution, have become FEARFUL, and turned back and settled down again in Babylon. In the Camp of the Saints located on top of Mt. Zion, the soul is fully satisfied, happy and free, "filled with all the fullness of God." Its elevation is high and healthy. The "ites" are all driven out. Its enemies are shooting at long range from the hills of Babylon. It is founded on God's mountain of truth. It is high, and far above the wisdom of men. It can ONLY be ascended by USE of the WINGS OF THE EVENING LIGHT. Its tables are filled with good things. "They shall hunger no more." A full table is set "in the presence of their enemies." They are fearless in battle and have accepted God as "the hope of His people." No battle is lost in the camp of the saints. You may lose by leaving the CAMP.

ALL that enter the "camp of the saints" must have on the whole armour of God. Half clad folks never get in. They have their loins girded about with truth. Their "feet are shod with the preparation of the gospel of peace." It is a sure and peaceable foundation on which to stand. The shield of faith is always in readiness to quench all the fiery darts of the wicked. The helmet of salvation becomes a wall around them. The Word of God is the sword of the Spirit that slays ALL that charge their ranks. This is the final BATTLE GROUND of the TRUE CHURCH OF GOD. It is in this place that the Bride will have made herself ready, and will take her final flight to meet Him in the air at His second coming.

I have laid much stress on the safety of those entering and staying in the camp of the saints. This is true. The devil will not be able to pluck those out of the hand of Jesus that determine to stay there. We want to notice another picture. It is a battle ground. It is a battle between truth and error, right against wrong, sin against holiness and righteousness. It is the devil and all false religions against God and true religion; the devil and his followers against God and His people. This is the "Battle of Armageddon."

For 270 years the morning church had victory; then followed the APOSTASY for 260 years, ending 530 A.D. During this age of apostasy, Satan succeeded in deceiving the nations of the world. From 530 to 1530 A.D. was a thousand years of extreme darkness. No new deceptions were brought on the people during this one thousand year period of time. In Rev. 20:3, it tells us what happened to the devil during this thousand years. "And cast him into the bottomless pit, and shut him up, and set a seal upon him, that he should deceive the nations NO MORE, till the thousand years should be finished: and after that he MUST be loosed a little season." This text makes it clear that there were no new deceptions introduced during this thousand year period. It was true that he deceived the nations on more until the thousand years were expired. During the 350 years of Protestant creed-making he was certainly loosed.

"And when the thousand years are expired, Satan shall be loosed out of his prison, and shall go out to deceive the nations which are in the four quarters of the earth, Gog and Magog, (Catholics and Protestants) to gather them to battle: the number of whom is as the sand of the sea. And they went upon the earth and compassed the camp of the saints about, and the beloved city: and fire came down from God out of heaven, and devoured them. And the devil that deceived them was cast into the lake of fire and brimstone, where the beast and false prophet are, and shall be tormented day and night forever and ever." Rev. 20:7-10.

Satan brought many deceptions during the Protestant age of 350 years. At the time of the beginning of the "evening light" the Gog and Magog powers of Catholicism and Protestantism were fully established. These two forces are gathering their powers together in the eighth beast of BABYLON THE GREAT, THE MOTHER OF HAR-LOTS, to compass the "camp of the saints about, and the beloved city." These all oppose the true Church that Jesus built, and the fundamental truths that characterize it. Who is able to count these multitudes who are as innumerable as the sand of the sea.

Now let us turn to Rev. 16:13-16 and see the kind of wicked spirits working in BABYLON THE GREAT today. "And I saw three unclean spirits like frogs come out of the mouth of the dragon, and out of the mouth of the beast, and out of the mouth of the false prophet. For they are the spirits of devils, working miracles, which go forth unto the kings of the earth and of the whole world, to gather them to battle of that great day of God Almighty. Behold, I come as a thief. Blessed is he that watcheth and keepeth his garments, lest he walk naked, and they see his shame. And he gathered them together into a place called in the Hebrew tongue Armageddon."

These first verses we quoted shows us three unclean spirits, like frogs, working in Babylon the Great. A frog is cold, slick, and slimy; so are the spirits. The spirit of the dragon is atheistic in its very nature. In many ways it denies God. It is plainly seen in Dr. Herbert Betts' report which he gave on the 700 ministers. We have previously given that report. Turn back and read it again, and you will see all of them denied the plain Word of God. This is the dragonistic, antichrist spirit working in Babylon today.

The spirit out of the mouth of the beast promotes all deceptive doctrines and practices of beast religion, branded Christian. This spirit is very prominently at work in Babylon. The spirit of the false prophet is seen in wildfire, false holiness movements, substituting the power of the devil for the power and gifts of the Spirit of God. Wherever these spirits work, it must be branded Babylon. Some have Church of God over the door of the church house, but plenty of Babylon practices on the inside.

In verse 14 we are plainly told that "these are spirits of devils, working miracles, which go forth unto the kings of the earth and to the whole world." The kings are the great religious leaders. They are deceived by the working of these spirits of devils, and it extends all over the world. They are on the devil's side, fighting against God and His truth. Many will not have God's truth. They refuse it and instead hold up their own doctrines. They are gathering all possible into their ranks, the number of whom is as the sand of the sea, fighting a losing battle against an ALL POWERFUL GOD.

It is a horrible picture when we see the great forces led by kings, captains, and many of less rank, marching in to worship God, and then see them operate under the working of the spirits of devils. They are promoting the devil's work, "deceiving and being deceived." The great majority of people in Babylon are not saved. They belong to something, but have never repented of their sins and do not know what the peace of God is.

In Rev. 16:19 we are told that the city of Babylon was divided into three parts. This division had reference to the working of the three unclean spirits. It says, "The cities of the nations fell," and means that they all became one great city by uniting all church movements together.

The move to federate all churches has made great progress in the past 20 years. There is a vast difference in UNION and UNITY. A form of union through federation is Babylon's substitute for BIBLE UNITY.

The Three Faiths Commission, whose objective is to unite Catholics, Protestants, and Jews, was started in 1937. Within a few years it had spread into the entire 48 states. In February, 1940, they participated in a national demonstration in more than 1000 towns and cities.

In 1938, the National Conference of Christians and Jews had set up its organizations in 310 cities, reached over 1000 college campuses, and over 200 daily newspapers subscribed to its services. Its radio recordings were heard regularly on many stations. Thousands of meetings are held in hundreds of communities in the 48 states, with an estimated 25,000 conferences. I am giving you these facts that you may see BABYLON THE GREAT, THE MOTHER OF HARLOTS, as she forms herself into the "Eighth beast" power through the process of uniting. It is ridiculous for people to think they can unite such ·UNSCRIPTURAL FAITHS as these, and make a Holy Bride for a Holy Christ. It is the purpose of the Gog and Magog powers to federate all deceptions to oppose the TRUTH. The Jews always have denied Christ. Their attitude toward Him has not changed since they crucified Him on the cross.

"And he gathered them together into a place called in the Hebrew tongue Armageddon." Rev. 16:16. The Gog and Magog forces are uniting, and we are now in that battle. Armageddon is a Hebrew word, the name of the battle field where many great battles of literal Israel were fought against their enemies. Both in gospel and the Revelation, the children of Israel are used as a symbol or a type of the church. They fought many battles on the plains of Megiddo. This was where Barack and Deborah won the battle against the Caananites. Judges 4. Later Gideon, with his reduced and tested few, won the great battle over the Midianites.

There are characteristics in the battles on the plains of Megiddo that we will find in the battle of Armageddon today. As long as Israel followed God's true prophet, they won the battles, but when they did evil in the sight of the Lord, they lost their battles. In most all places they were led to evil by their leaders. Some would get their eyes on the spoils of the battle, while others would covet the place and honor of leadership, and lead a revolt.

God has a people today who are using the WORD of God as their weapon, and are marching into Armageddon against the combined forces of Babylon the Great, THE MOTHER OF HARLOTS. Israel had traitors in the camp who led revolts; so do we. Israel had men seeking the spoils and aspiring to high places; so do we. The worst enemies Israel had were those of their own ranks WHO DID EVIL. There are many today who claim to stand for the truth that cannot be trusted. According to their works and fruits, they are a part of Babylon. When tested by the true Word of God, it can be easily seen what army they are fighting in.

Gideon's army who fought on the plains of Megiddo was a type of God's people today. Judges 7 and 8 gives an account of the 32,000 he started out with. God told Gideon he had too many men and to let all that were fearful and afraid turn back. We notice that 22,000 left the ranks of battle. In this great battle of Armageddon which we are in today, God is letting those who are "fearful and afraid" turn back. This is not compulsory, for God does not draft His soldiers of the cross. The call is to "whosoever will" accept ALL the truth of God's Word and stand against ALL sin and deceptions. The "evening light" is sparkling with gems of the fullness of everlasting truth. God is calling for volunteers who will don the whole armour of God, step into the ranks of His blood-washed, and be true to the end.

God wants a tried people. If you decide to stay in the battle, God will put you through a test. We notice in Judges 7:4 that God made the standard by which they were tested, and only 300 out of the remaining 10,000 passed the test. God has prescribed the standard today, and none dare change it. There was less than one percent who stood the test. Of all the thousands today professing to be true people of God, just a few will stand against all decptions, and for the truth, and cry, "Babylon is fallen, is fallen," and "Come out of her, my people."

There are just two general classes of professors of Christianity. One class is small in number, WALKING IN ALL THE LIGHT THEY HAVE, AND READY FOR MORE LIGHT WHEN IT COMES. The other class is large in number, many of whom never had the "born again" experience; others had it, but lost it because they refused to walk in the light they had. The large number of the "fearful" that turned back never had anything to lose, but those that did have salvation, lost it WHEN THEY TURNED BACK. Those that fail in the test will fail in the judgment. The FEW that stand true are, symbolically, said to be in the "Camp of the saints." Not many will qualify for a soldier in this great battle of Armageddon. The Babylonian forces to face are overwhelming in number. Gideon's 300 men defeated the 135,000 Midianites.

With many the price is too great to pay. They have relatives, friends, and boosters in Babylon with whom they will not break. Many leaders, whom John the Revelator calls "kings and captains," who hold offices and places of honor and salaries in Babylon, will not give them up. They

teach deceit and many of the lower rank "would have it so."
The outcome of this battle is determined by the quality
and not the quantiy of men.

This gospel differentiating between THE D I V I N E
CHURCH OF GOD and Babylon must be preached to
all the world. Those who profess Christ will be forced to
take their stand on one side or the other. If they go against
light, they will backslide—if they had anything to backslide from. At the present time there are not many saved
people left in Babylon.

"And he cried mightily with a strong voice saying,
Babylon the Great is fallen, is fallen, and is become the
habitation of devils, and the hold of every foul spirit, and
a cage of every unclean and hateful bird. For all nations
have drunk of the wine of the wrath of her fornication,
and the kings of the earth have waxed rich through the
abundance of her delicacies." Rev. 18:3-4. Dear saint, who
wants to stay with this kind of people? "And I heard another voice from heaven saying, Come out of her, my people, that ye be not partakers of her sins, and that ye receive not of her plagues." Verse 4. That other voice is the
Holy Spirit speaking. He will speak to SAINTS and
SAINTS can understand His message. When the Word
is preached and He says come out, and then you refuse,
you cease to be SAINTS. To fail to obey this voice of
the Holy Spirit means to cease to be a child of God. Many
refuse to obey God and are zealous promoters of Babylon.
Kings and captains spend much time in making up pro-
grams, organizing forces, raising budgets, and sending their
own type of missionaries WITHOUT THE APPROVAL
OF GOD UPON THEM. They "know not that they are
wretched, miserable, naked, blind, and destitute." Rev. 3:17.

In Rev. 18:5 we are told the reasons why we should
come out of Babylon: "For her sins have reached unto

heaven, and God hath remembered her iniquities." In the "dark and cloudy day" God is remembering her sins and dealing out His judgments against them. "Reward her even as she rewarded you, and double unto her double according to her works; in the cup which she hath filled fill unto her double." Verse 6. In the sixth seal God gave Babylon her FIRST cup of his judgments, and a tenth of the city fell. In the sounding of the seventh trumpet she is getting her second cup, and Babylon goes down to rise no more.

Now let us read the rest of this 18th chapter.

This seventh verse tells us how the people in Babylon praise, esteem, and honor this harlot woman as a queen. They say she is no widow. She claims Christ as her living husband. She did not realize that the judgments or plagues of God would bring sorrow to her people. Verse 8, "Therefore shall her plagues come in one day, death, and mourning, and famine; and she shall be utterly burned with fire: for strong is the Lord God who judges her."

We are told that the judgments of God against Babylon would come in a day. This is symbolic language, and the DAY covers the "Evening light" period of 100 years, through which God is burning Babylon with His judgment fires of truth. Those who desire to stay in Babylon after they hear God's message of truth will die spiritually. There will be a famine and people will mourn about it. Those who have made merchandise of their religion certainly will not want to see it destroyed. They will flee from the judgment fire of truth that destroys them, "When they shall see the smoke of their burning, standing afar off for fear of her torment, saying, Alas, alas, that great city Babylon, that mighty city! for in one hour is thy judgments come. And the merchants of the earth shall weep and mourn over her; for no man buyeth their merchandise any more." Rev. 18:10-11.

According to this scripture, the hour is coming when the judgments sent on Babylon will be so horrible that no man will want to buy their cheap, shoddy religion.

According to the 11th chapter of Daniel, in the last days "The King of the south," which is the power of Babylon the Great, "shall be strong, and one of his princes; . . . And in the end of years they shall join themselves together (Council of Churches); for the king's daughter (Protestantism) of the south shall come to the king of the north to make an agreement; but she shall not retain the power of the arm; neither shall he stand, nor his arm: but she shall be given up, and they that brought her, and he that begat her, and he that strengthened her in these times." Dan. 11:5-6.

In this scripture the king of the south is used to represent all beast religions. They. have become strong and are joining themselves together in the Council of Churches. The harlot daughters of Babylon the Great are making a league with the cold, icy, atheistic, Communistic powers of the north, filling their schools, seminaries ,and literature with faith-killing doctrines and theories. And through this, she is losing the power of her arm. Those signs that Jesus said would follow them that believe have disappeared.

By reading the rest of the 11th and 12th chapters of Daniel, you will see there is a battle being fought between the king of the south and the king of the north. The world is divided into two great forces today. One is trying to annihilate all religions; the other is trying to sustain all religions. These two forces meet face to face around the table of the U. N. "And both these kings' hearts shall be to do mischief, and they shall speak lies at one table: but it shall not prosper, for yet the end shall be at the appointed time." Dan. 11:27. From now on to the end of time these two powers or kings shall be in battle against each other. The king of the south gathers her princes into Egypt's bondage to her gods of religions, while the king of the north gathers his forces to destroy and bring a complete annihilation of all religions.

The battle is raging with each side surging for victory. In Dan. 11:9-11, we read that the king of the south, which is Babylon the Great, sets forth a great multitude, only for them to be given into the hands of the king of the north. In verse 12, we see how the king of the north is lifted up by his victory and casts down many ten thousands. In verse 13 we see how in a few years the king of the north comes with greater multitudes and carries away great riches. Verse 15, "So the king of the north shall come and cast up a mount, and take the most fenced cities: and the armies of the south shall not withstand." Verse 16, "But he that cometh against him shall do according to his own will, and none shall stand before him; and he (king of the north) shall stand in the glorious land, (the true people of God) which by his hand shall be consumed." Verse 17, "He shall set his face to enter with the strength of his whole kingdom, and upright ones with him: thus shall he do: and he shall give him the daughters of women, (Babylon) corrupting her, but she shall not stand on his side." Verse 18, "After this shall he turn his face unto the isles, and shall take many: but a prince (Jesus) for his own behalf shall cause the reproach offered by him (King of the north) to cease; without his own reproach he shall cause it to turn upon him." Verse 19, "Then he (king of the north) shall turn his face toward the fort of his own land: and he shall stumble and fall and not be found."

We see according to the above scriptures that the king of the north is, as he nears the end of time, making an all-out move to destroy all religions, even to destroy the true people of God. Jesus referred to this great tribulation in Matt. 24:21-22, "For then shall be great tribulation, such as was not since the beginning of the world to this time, no nor ever shall be. And except those days be shortened, there should no flesh be saved: but for the elect's sake those days shall be shortened." He surely means that unless God shortens the days of the great slaughter, there will be no Christians left in the flesh when Jesus comes at the end. He declares that for the elect's sake those days will be shortened. At this time the king of the north will think he is winning a great victory, "but he shall stumble and fall, and not be found." It will certainly be no reproach to Jesus Christ to stop this great battle and slaughter at his second coming.

I do not have space for all of this from the book of Daniel, but the rest which I did not read will harmonize with the thoughts I have given. You may study it for yourself. To show you that the devil will not be satisfied to stop with the destruction of the forces of the king of the south, which is Babylon, let us read Dan. 11:45, "And he (king of the north) shall plant the tabernacle of his palace between the seas in the glorious holy mountain; yet he shall come to his end, and none shall help him." This once more brings us to the end of time.

Dan. 12:1 once more tells us of the conditions at the end of time. "And at that time shall Michael stand up, the great prince (Jesus), which standeth for the children of thy people: and there shall be a time of trouble, such as never was since there was a nation even to that same time: and at that time thy people shall be delivered, every one that shall be found written in the book." Daniel uses the same words as Jesus when he says such a time of trouble "never was." This brings us to the end of time, for the next verse says, "And many of them that sleep in the dust of the earth shall awake . . . ."

I am giving you the sketches of the battle between the king of the north, pershaps Communism and its satellite forces, and the king of the south, which is "BABYLON THE GREAT, THE MOTHER OF HARLOTS." The final outcome is that Babylon the Great, king of the south, goes down to rise no more at all. The devil is the author of Babylon for the purpose of deceiving people, but now is ready to destroy his own work in order to destroy all religions. This is nothing new, for in many places in the Old Bible God permits the devil and his forces to bring judgments on Israel because of her sins.

Some may say that this kind of an ending seems to be victory for the devil, when God must shorten time in order to have any saints left on the earth when Jesus comes. The gospel will have been preached to all the world. Multitudes, multitudes will have been in the valley of decision. Babylon will have been judged and is fallen, and is without scriptural foundation. All those that want to obey God's call will have come out. God lets the devil strike the final blow at his own work. Then the devil turns on God's elect. He brings a halt to it all, with the greatest victory that ever came. The greatest battle will bring the greatest victory. There never has been a greater victory than will be at the second coming of Christ, when all the teeming millions that sleep in the dust shall rise in immortality. If that is the greatest tribulation that ever has been, then the saints will SHINE the brightest of all ages, with the greatest victory.

Now let us do a little summing up: the king of the south is Babylon the Great, the Mother of Harlots, the eighth beast. She is operated and run by three unclean spirits like frogs. "And is become the habitation of devils, and the hold of every foul spirit, and a cage of every unclean and hateful bird." The king of the north represents the spirit of the devil working with his cold, icy hand to destroy all religions, even the "holy people." All of these Satantic powers are in opposition to the truth of God's Word. They are surrounding the camp of the saints in the great battle of ARMAGEDDON.

We are told in Rev. 18:8, in speaking of Babylon, that "her plagues shall come in one day," meaning 100 years of "evening light" pouring out the judgments of God against her. The angel that sounded this trumpet said, "Babylon is FALLEN"—SPIRITUALLY, SHE HAS LOST EVERY-THING. But she is still here in existence carrying on in a fallen condition spiritually. In verse 9 we read, "For in one hour is thy judgment come." This hour shows her final destruction. Verse 17, "For in one hour is so great riches come to naught." This one hour brings the complete annihilation of BABYLON THE GREAT through the forces of the king of the north. The sounding of the seventh trumpet (God's message of truth) brings her spiritual fall and the opposing dragon powers of the king of the north brings her physical and final destruction in a short period of time called "an hour." This hour of great tribulation is about seven years and Jesus said for the "elects'" sake it shall be shortened. This tells us that this great tribulation will not last a full hour but will be cut short for the elects' sake.

The sounding of the seventh trumpet and the opening of the seventh seal cover the same period of time, for it is the sounding of the trumpet that opens the mysteries of the seal. "And when he had opened the seventh seal, there was silence in heaven (the church) about the space of an half hour." Rev. 8:1. As long as the trumpet was sound-ing, there would not be silence. When the trumpet, God's message of truth, stops sounding, THAT BRINGS SI-LENCE in heaven, the church. The king of the north will have not only succeeded in destroying Babylon, but also "planted his tabernacle in the glory land," the true church. When the king of the north, which is the dragon powers, gets the throttle of the world in his hands, all religion stops, including the true religion. This brings silence in heaven, the church. John, the Revelator, says this silence is for "about an half hour." This corresponds with the shortening of time for the elects' sake.

Bear this in mind that the true saints of God will not stop their worship and service to God. They will not hesitate to break the commandments of the king of the north. This will bring persecution and slaughter, which will call for a shortening of time for the elects' sake. But the gospel to the unsaved world will practically cease. In Matt. 24:20 Jesus says, "Pray that your flight (out of Babylon) be not in the winter time." This period of about an half hour of silence is winter time brought about by the king of the north. Those that hear that other voice saying, "Come out of her, my people," had better heed before winter time comes. When persecution becomes so strong that such a time never has been, it will be a difficult time to obey the voice of the Lord and come out of Babylon.

Babylon is carrying on in a great way and will continue in the sale of her merchandise of false religions through the entire age of the seventh seal. The seventh trumpet message of truth is dealing out the judgments of God, burning her with Holy Spirit fire, yet she is going on with her work of abomination, selling her merchandise in a greater way than ever before. The Council of Churches is reaching many nations today and gathering multitudes into its abominable deceptions. In the realm of BABYLON THE GREAT we still hear occasionally the voice of the Bridegroom. There are some that still preach some of the Bible. We can still hear this voice occasionally in some of the so-called holiness movements. We still hear occasionally the voice of a saint over in Babylon who has not found his way out, but the time is coming when people will no longer buy their religious wares that do not satisfy the soul. "And the merchants of the earth shall weep and mourn over her; for no man buyeth their merchandise any more." Rev. 18: 11. The next few verses tell us what has happened to Babylon the Great and when it came.

"The merchandise of gold, and of silver, and of precious stones, and of pearl, and of fine linen, and purple, and silk, and scarlet, and all thyine wood, and all manner vessels of ivory, and all manner vessels of most precious wood, and of brass, and of iron, and marble, and cinnamon, and odours, and ointments, and frankincense, and wine, and oil, and fine flour, and wheat, and beasts, and sheep, and horses, and chariots, and slaves, and souls of men. And the fruits that thy soul lusted after are departed from thee, and all things which were dainty and goodly are departed from thee, AND THOU SHALT FIND THEM NO MORE AT ALL." Rev. 18:12-14. After the above mentioned things are all departed from Babylon, it seems certain that no one will want to buy what is left. Let us read verse 15. "The merchants of THESE THINGS (above mentioned), which were made rich by her, shall stand afar off for the FEAR OF HER TORMENT, weeping and wailing. And saying, Alas, alas, that great city (Babylon), that was clothed in fine linen, and purple, and scarlet, and decked with gold, and precious stones, and pearls!" Verse 17, "FOR IN ONE HOUR so great riches is come to nought. And every shipmaster, and all the company in ships, and sailors, and as many as trade by sea, stood afar off." This verse 17 tells us when this will all take place. Remember we are dealing with symbols, and the Holy Spirit must help us to interpret their meaning. This is that short period of time when the king of the north sets his hand to make the final destruction of the king of the south with all religions. People of Babylon will have to recant, give

up their religions or march to the concentration camp or
before the firing squad. Men will not give their head for
a religion that does not go beneath the collar bone. This
will test the consecration of the most consecrated. Perhaps some of the saints will undertake to save their lives
and lose them. Some are looking for a great revival. How
do we know but what this will bring it. It is said that the
morning church THRIVED ON THE BLOOD OF ITS
MARTYRS. I am persuaded that when this time comes
we will see the power of God manifested in a wonderful
way, and signs and wonders wrought as we have not seen
them. This will win people to God who can't be reached
any other way. Only the true saints of God will stand for
truth in the face of death.

At this time the true people of God will all have had
the truth preached to them and will have seen the wickedness of Babylon—that she is the hold of every foul spirit,
and the cage of every hateful and unclean bird, and will
flee to Mt. Sion, into the camp of the saints. The coveteous,
crafty kings and captains of Babylon will cry and bewail
themselves when they see their merchandise of churchanity
being destroyed. "Saying, Alas, alas, that great city, where-
in were made rich all that had ships in the sea by reason
of her costliness! for in ONE HOUR is she made desolate."
Rev. 18:19.

Those who love Babylon will cry and lament over her
destruction, but those that have obeyed God's command to
"Come out of her, MY pepole," are commanded to "rejoice." Those who love Babylon can't do this. People
cannot rejoice over the destruction of a thing that they
love. "Rejoice over her, thou heaven, and ye holy apostles
and prophets; for God hath avenged (past tense) you on
her." It has already been accomplished spiritually. Babylon has been guilty of spiritual and literal martyrdom of
thousands of God's people in the past. She is a harlot and

a murderer. "And I saw the woman drunk with the blood of the saints, and of the blood of the martyrs of Jesus." Rev. 17:6. "And the woman that thou sawest is the great city (Babylon) which reigneth over the kings of the earth." Rev. 17:18. IF BABYLON THE GREAT, THE MOTHER OF HARLOTS, is this kind of character, we should rejoice at her execution under the righteous judgments of God. "Vengeance is mine; I will repay, saith the Lord." If God's righteous judgment calls for her destruction, we should rejoice when it is done. The saints love the souls of men, even though they are down in Babylon. They want to see them blessed of God—that is why they are making that clarion cry, "BABYLON IS FALLEN, IS FALLEN" and "COME OUT OF HER, MY PEOPLE."

Let us turn to Rev. 18:21 and read some more about this final destruction of Babylon. "And a mighty angel took up a stone like a great millstone, and cast it into the sea, saying, Thus with violence shall that great city Babylon be thrown down, and shall be found no more at all." This scripture tells us the manner of the destruction of Babylon. The violent hand of the king of the north, that old atheistic, communistic spirit of the dragon, will complete her destruction, then Michael, the great prince, will cut the time short, and deliver His people by bringing an end to it all.

Let us notice some more of what John says about this shortened hour of destruction. "And the voice of harpers, and musicians, and pipers, and trumpeters, shall be heard no more at all in thee: and no craftsman of whatsoever craft he be, shall be found any more in thee; and the sound of a millstone shall be heard no more at all in thee. And the light of a candle shall shine no more at all in thee: and the voice of the bridegroom and the bride shall be heard no more at all in thee: for thy merchants were the great men of the earth; for by thy sorceries were all nations deceived. And in her (Babylon) was found the blood of prophets, and of saints, and of all that were slain upon the earth." Rev. 18:22-24.

These scriptures are just re-affirming to us the stopping of the preaching of the gospel during this period of "about half an hour" of silence. The voice of harpers, musicians, pipers and trumpeters have reference to kings and captains selling their religious wares of merchandise. The voice of the bridegroom will not be heard. This means there will be no gospel preached any more at all in Babylon. There will be no saved people letting their light shine in Babylon, for she has gone down to rise NO MORE. And once more we have the charges laid to her account: "For by thy sorceries were all nations deceived."

Surely there has been enough said that people of average intelligence can see what BABYLON is. We have proven it by the Bible, history and present day happenings. Dear reader, you may not understand it all, but you have gotten points of truth that lay a responsibility on you, and YOU MUST MAKE A DECISION. You must accept it or reject it. With many, their treasure in Babylon is their God. They love its association and merchandise and its wealth which are perishable. Babylon offers much to the satisfying of the flesh and little to satisfying of the soul. It robs God, Jesus, and the Holy Spirit of their rightful place in our worship service. Well, these things have all been made plain.

Light is come. God's will is made clear. That "other voice" has said, "Come out of her, my people." The devil comes at this point of time, and lays before us his last trap in the form of a "delusion." Perhaps he may first show you some magnified values of Babylon and tell you that "You just can't afford to give them up." He will tell you that you can preach some truth and yet stay in Babylon and that will be sufficient. He will tell you just to not preach that truth that exposes Babylon and her deceptions and sins, because that will cause her "kings and captains" to kick you out and you will become an outcast. His argument is to get you to believe that you can get by without OBEYING ALL THE TRUTH OF GOD. Through his magnified flatteries he will cause you to love some things in Babylon more than you love God's truth. In this way he pulls the trigger of his trap and you become one of those people spoken of in II Thess. 2:10-12. "And with all deceivableness of unrighteousness in them that perish; BECAUSE THEY RECEIVED NOT THE LOVE FOR THE TRUTH, that they might be saved. AND FOR THIS CAUSE GOD shall send them strong delusion, that they might all be damned who believed not the truth, but had pleasure in unrighteousness." The above described people are not a FEW in number, but many. Many are honest enough to acknowledge the thing they are associated with is not right, yet that love for something it has, keeps them tied and bound in its bondage. Some ministers preach a clean life and holy living but will not preach against the ecclesiastical hierarchy ruling the movement, feeding themselves and not the flock. It takes courage to tell people that they are in Babylon, and GOD SAID to "Have no fellowship with the unfruitful works of darkness," and to "Come out of her, my people." This means a break with the old group. Many preachers can boldly say, "Thou shalt not steal," but are void of that LOVE FOR TRUTH and are fearful to CRY OUT against the sins of THEIR OWN PEOPLE. The position many take is plain and simple: they LOVE THE UNSCRIPTURAL PRACTICES IN THEIR MOVEMENT MORE THAN THEY LOVE THE WORD OF GOD THAT SAYS, "COME OUT OF IT." God did not say to REFORM BABYLON and WORK HER OVER, AND I'LL ACCEPT HER. I have heard this expression by many: "If we will stay in there

(Babylon), we can reform it." This is not God's way. Even a reformed BABYLON will always be a HARLOT. "Let him that is in the field not turn back to get anything out of his house." Matt. 24:17. Some say that they are working in Babylon, going along trying to get some good to them. In order to do this, you will have to preach a weak, diluted message, condone sin, and support deception with your TIME AND MONEY. Why waste our TIME AND MONEY BUYING RECOGNITION IN BABYLON THE GREAT, THE MOTHER OF HARLOTS?

Some have said, "If we do not support missionaries, how can the world be saved?" Friend, remember this, Babylon cannot save the world with its diluted and weakened message. She sends her OWN kind of missionaries, who preach her OWN doctrines, bringing her adherents into bondage to her own ecclesiastical hierarchy. BABYLON does not have the message that it takes to save the world. IT TAKES A FULL MESSAGE TO BRING FULL SALVATION. God's way is, COME OUT OF BABYLONIAN BONDAGE AND BE FREE, AND TAKE THE WHOLE TRUTH TO THE WHOLE WORLD. God has said in plain language that "BABYLON IS FALLEN," yet many support her budgets regularly. Her kings and captains are still wanting to accumulate riches. Why support and stay in a thing that is FALLEN? That is foolish and extremely unwise; but the devil says to do it, because there is good there yet. Anyone who has any intelligence at all would leave a building that was falling down. Yet the devil has many under his FREE-LOVE delusion, so blinded that they cannot see their BABYLONIAN structure is "FALLEN." This is spiritual FREE-LOVE. No man wants his bride to place her affections on some one else. Neither does Jesus want His bride, the church, to place her love and affections on any movement in Babylon. Instead He wants them to RETAIN A LOVE for Him and His truth.

The devil calms some people's spiritual nerves by telling them to be calm, and don't say anything bad about the religion of others. If they are religious, just love them and call them brother; tell them to be faithful in whatever they believe. Jesus did not do this. He called black, black and white, white. He said, "Woe unto you, Pharisees, hypocrites," while many today would say, "God bless you, BROTHER, just keep on professing." Jesus had the kind of LOVE we should have. The FREE-LOVER will love anything that comes along. The kind of love God gives causes us to LOVE GOD WITH ALL OUR HEARTS, and hate SIN and deception like God hates it. If we love our neighbor as ourselves we will want him to have the same kind of love we have, and will WARN HIM against a substitute suggested by the devil. If we have the pure love of God in our hearts, we will not be glad that people are in sin and deception, but we will love to tell its follies and the BETTER WAY. God's love makes us LOVE AND ENJOY PREACHING THE GOSPEL TO ALL OF THE WORLD. We will never win people to the truth by COMPROMISING A N D SUPPORTING T H E I R DECEPTIONS.

When I was a small boy I got saved. They told me that I should join the church. I did what they told me to do, not knowing the Bible was against such things. I went to reading my Bible in search of truth. I soon saw that their doctrines were twisted and warped. They told me that I could not lose it. If I lost it, I never had it, and if I kept it, I could not live it. I was just a small school boy, but I knew this was not right. I was bold in telling my convictions. They said they did not want any boy in their church that believed in holiness, and turned me out. They said that they sinned every day. After I was out, and began to look the thing over, I decided they had told the truth. Well, thank God, I soon found the glorious Church of God. I saw a church divine in its origin, organization and operation, one whose articles of faith, by-laws, and code of operation is the WORD OF GOD. I saw a church divinely organized, equipped with the gifts of the Spirit, with authority and power to carry out the GREAT COM- MISSION. "And God set the members in the body (the church) as it pleased him." I Cor. 12:18. "And he is the head of the body, the church: who is the beginning, the first born from the dead; THAT IN ALL THINGS HE MIGHT HAVE THE PREEMINENCE." Col. 1:18. These scriptures tell us the BODY is the CHURCH, and Christ is the HEAD of the body. The head should rule the body, and not some organized group of its members. Christ is only head of that group who willingly seeks and follows his direction. The only headquarters the Church of God has, or needs, is in heaven where Christ, the head of the church, is seated. Jesus said, "All power is given unto me." "Behold, I send you . . ." "Go ye therefore . . ." "What- soever ye shall ask in my name I will do it . . ." "I give you power. . ." "Ye shall tread on serpents . . ." "Go ye therefore into all the world and preach the gospel to every creature. He that believeth and is baptized shall be saved; but he that believeth not shall be damned. And these signs shall follow them that believe; in my name shall they cast out devils; they shall speak with new tongues; they shall take up serpents; and if they drink any deadly thing it shall not hurt them; they shall lay hands on the sick and they shall recover." Mark 16:15-18. "Go ye therefore and teach all nations, baptizing them in the name of the Father, and of the Son, and of the Holy Ghost: teaching them to ob- serve all things whatsoever I have commanded you: and, lo, I am with you alway, even unto the end of the world." Matt. 28:19-20. This commission is perfect, complete, eco- nomical and efficient. Man can add nothing to its perfec- tion. Anything that man would tie on would become a dead weight, an overhead expense. Surely, if we will get close enough to God for Him to open our spiritual eyes, that we may see this glorious divinely organized group of people, there will be no place for man's organizations and churches.

There is much sin and deception covered up in money raising schemes in Babylon. Gospel giving is a Bible doctrine and has its place in the church. We are agreed that missionaries have needs we can supply, but it is the wrong way of raising money, and the use that is made of it, that I want to speak of. The Bible tells us that it is more blessed to give than to receive, but covetous people would much rather have it the other way. Real saints will not shut up their bowels of compassion against their brother when they see him in need. God works on the inside, but man has devised ways to work on the outside. God's way of supporting His people is through faith and trust in Him. Prayer, faith, and trust for financial and physical needs are a wonderful asset to spiritual success. Man's systems of raising money and supporting the church robs men of the use of faith in God; then God is robbed of the glory in answering the prayer of faith. There is very little unnecessary overhead expense to get help from God through the prayer of faith. God's way eliminates the unnecessary expense of transportation by the covetous man.

In man's quest to raise money, he will use most any system that will get it. The Bible strongly supports the FREE-WILL OFFERING PLAN, but many times it is HIGH-PRESSURED. The free-will offerings of those void of salvation in their hearts are small.

Man has devised a multiplicity of organized systems to support the church. Any human organization brings bondage, and all must adopt it whether they like it or not. They show a lack of understanding of God's way or faith to carry it out. Organization calls for an executive force which must first be paid out of the funds they succeed in getting. Church Extension, Home and Foreign Missionary Boards hestitate to tell the overhead expense of SALARIES and OFFICE UPKEEP. Amount of salary paid for certain offices seems to be somewhat a secret. This leaves people wondering.

Church boards and committees are, like man-made churches, soon filled with unsaved people. The covetous and selfish man soon begins to lay plans and schemes to fill his own coffers. It is not an uncommon thing to hear of money scandals; however, they usually try to cover them up. We are not trying to say that all these men are rascals, or even unsaved, but the saved who are there must work with just that kind of people.

The organization of such boards and committees soon develop into a headquarters of power and authority. Certain plans and policies develop which call for the extension of the executive force whose salaries and expenses must be paid. These methods are unscriptural. They cause excessive expense and open the door for unsaved people to hold offices and operate in the work of the church. This is not Biblical and belongs to Babylon. God does not give unsaved men high offices in His church. God does not authorize the creation of such offices because He knew the kings and captains would become corrupt and oppress the people. God's plan is holy, and he calls for holy men to carry it out. He does not set the unholy in "the body, the Church." The unholy are not endowed with the gifts of the Spirit and the power to carry out the commission with signs following. God does not call and send the unholy to carry out the great commission, for they would be faithless, powerless and fruitless. If any real good is accomplished, it will not be their faith that does it. Only the saved and holy have any place in God's Church. There are many who do not see the mode of membership and plan of operation in the Church that Jesus built. There are many saved people who do not have a VISION of the Bible Church of God. As a result, they fall in line with Babylon. When people fall in line with man-made by-laws, and the formulating of organizations to carry out their own ritualistic beliefs, they have set up something that the unsaved can operate in. Then the holy must be tolerant toward the UNHOLY and call them BROTHER. Light has no fellowship with darkness. To KNOWINGLY mix it, will put out the light. It is IMPOSSIBLE for a man to set up ANY KIND of a church organization AND KEEP IT CLEAN. If God could have His way, the unsaved would have no part in the spiritual work of the church. If the saved people will follow the WORD AND SPIRIT and refuse to recognize the profession of the unsaved and unholy, God will have a HOLY CHURCH. But when the majority of a congregation is unsaved, the minority will have carnal wranglings and Babylonian rules and practices. The changing and reforming power is in the hands of those who will not reform. It is a hopeless case, but God has a way for His people to get out of such unholy bondage. "Come out of her, my people," Rev. 18:4. "Be ye not unequally yoked together with unbelievers: for what fellowship hath righteousness with unrighteousness? and what communion hath light with darkness? and what concord hath Christ with Belial? or what part hath he that believeth with an infidel? And what agreement hath the temple of God with (Babylon) idols? for ye are the temple of the living God, as God hath said, I will dwell in them, and walk in them; and I will be their God and they shall be my people. Wherefore come out from among them, and be ye separate saith the Lord, and touch not the unclean thing, and I will receive you; and will be a Father unto you, and ye shall be my sons and my daughters, saith the Lord Almighty." II Cor. 6:13-18.

The first verse says to be not unequally yoked together with unbelievers. If you are yoked at all, it is an unequal yoke. The thing Paul describes will always be found among the unsaved wherever they are found playing church. The saints of God do not have fellowship with such things. If they are forced to try, they will get spiritually sick, and if something is not done about it, they will die. Babylon today is so overwhelmingly run by unsaved people, and is so filled with spiritual cholera, that saints must change climates, and MOVE OUT ON HIGH, HEALTHY, SUNNY MT. SION, or be numbered with the DEAD. If we are the temple of God and God dwells in us, walks in us, and we are His people, and He is our God, will He withhold any good thing from him that walketh uprightly? Can we not, as His ministry and Church, get DIVINE directions on ALL THINGS? The distance to travel is shorter because He dwells in our hearts. His decisions are safer because He is the source of ALL WISDOM. We are directly connected to Christ, the head of the body, the Church, and it is natural and normal for the members to be directed by the head. In verses 17 and 18, which we just read, God has made a promise that takes care of everything we need. He said, "I will receive you," and "I will be a FATHER unto you, and ye shall be my sons and daughters." If ye "Come out from among them, and be ye separate, saith the Lord, and touch not the unclean thing; and I will RECEIVE YOU." People who do this, DO NOT HAVE to go to BABYLON for its unsafe advice or bogus religious wares. Some saints in the past, in spite of Babylonian bondage and its lords, have trusted God and received answer to prayer. After we see the plain commands of God and refuse to obey, our faith will be gone and we can no longer touch the hem of His garment. When one decides to fail God, they go under a "delusion"; then it will not be hard to fall in line with Babylon's dead, lifeless, formalities and call them Brother.

Now when God said for us to "Come out of her, my people," He did not mean for us to stay in it. He means for us to separate ourselves from it—be separate. This means to get out and stay away. If this woman is the kind of character she is described to be in Rev. 17, we had better flee from her spiritual fornications. We know it is not safe to habitually hang around people of a bad character. No one is out of Babylon who loves her success, and supports any phase of her operations. God's people LOVE to see lost souls saved, but have a sad feeling of regret when they see them yoking up in Babylonian bondage.

You just cannot stay in Babylon very long and preach ALL THE WORD OF GOD. It does not fit in their program, and it will condemn much of their operation and way of living. If you do not willingly depart "out of their coasts," the synagogues will soon be closed. In the minds of those who love Babylon you will be considered an "OUT-CAST." This means to be despised, hated, persecuted, frowned upon, and many times lied upon; yes, "despisers of those that are good."

"And it shall come to pass in that day, that the great trumpet shall be blown, and they shall come which were ready to perish in the land of Assyria, and the OUTCASTS in the land of Egypt, and shall worship the Lord in the holy mountain of Israel." Isa. 27:13. This is a prophecy to be fulfilled in the last part of the gospel day. The great trumpet is the seventh and last trumpet, which is sounding at this present time. It is during the sounding of this great trumpet that the people perishing in Assyria, the country where Babylon is located, may return and worship the Lord in the holy mount at Jerusalem. Egypt means bondage of

Babylon, and those in this bondage who are willing to become "OUTCASTS" shall worship God in His holy mountain in "the heavenly Jerusalem." It is the OUTCASTS that God can lead into His holy mountain. Those who are not willing to become OUTCASTS for the sake of the TRUTH will not be led out of this Egyptian bondage of Babylon into God's glorious Mount Sion Church.

Some people fight HOLINESS, others fight FAITH AND MIRACLES, while others fight a DIVINE CHURCH AND DIVINE GOVERNMENT in the church, either by word or practice. They make OUTCASTS, or cast those out who do not go along with them. "And he shall set up an ensign (a standard) for the nations, and shall assemble the OUTCASTS OF ISRAEL, and gather together the dispersed (scattered) of Judah from the four corners of the earth." Isa. 11:12.

In the sounding of the seventh and great trumpet, God is setting up an "ensign," meaning a standard for the nations to go by. And through the preaching of the FULL standard of His truth, He is ASSEMBLING those who are OUTCASTS of Babylon. It is only a remnant that will be ASSEMBLED in the great Mount Sion Church of God. This "gathering together" is not geographical, as some teach, but it is gathering to God's Mount Sion of Holiness and TRUTH of a DIVINE CHURCH.

"And it shall come to pass in that day, that the Lord shall set his hand again the second time to recover the remnant of his people, which shall be left, from Assyria, and from Egypt, and from Pathros, and from Cush, and from Elam, and from Shinar, and from Hamath, and from the islands of the sea." Isa. 11:11. This scripture is telling us that God will set His hand "AGAIN THE SECOND TIME" to gather a "REMNANT" of His people. He set his hand the FIRST TIME in the sixth seal. He gathered a great number symbolized by "an hundred and forty and four thousand." Rev. 14:1. That same movement that came out of Babylon, clear and clean, and were the Mt. Sion Church in the sixth seal, have gone back to practicing the VERY THING they came out of. This movement became a part of Babylon. And now God is "setting His hand again the SECOND TIME" to recover a REMNANT of His people. It is just a remnant, just those who are willing to become "outcasts," will hear "that other voice," to "Come out," and let God do the assembling or setting in the Body, the Church, as it pleases Him. This kind of an OUTCAST has a pure, holy, sincere, devoted spirit of love, faith, and zeal for God and His TRUTH. Surely God CAN LEAD this kind of people. "The Lord doeth BUILD UP JERUSALEM: he gathereth together the OUT-CASTS OF ISRAEL; he healeth the broken in heart, and bindeth up their wounds.", Psa. 147;2-3.

This is indeed the SOUNDING OF A GREAT TRUM-PET. It will awake the sleeping nations to see the reality of God's judgments against Babylon, and truth of His glorious assembled, unified church located ONCE MORE on Mount Sion. Of course, the Babylonian nations will be angry, and make OUTCASTS of those who "Follow the Lamb whithersoever He goeth." God's true people are said to be, in symbolic language, "gathered into the camp of the saints." We are to walk in the light, ascend God's glorious Mount Sion of truth, pitch our tents in the "camp of the saints," get hold of this GREAT TRUMPET, blow it until Babylon breaks "to shivers," and God's glorious church is shining like the "sun in the kingdom of our God."

There are some noted theologians today who see this divided and confused condition and acknowledge that it is not scriptural. They say that conditions are getting better as time goes on, that God somehow will bring all movements to the Bible standard, and we will then have unity, all speaking the same thing. Some look for a gradual elimination of error and deception and a restoration of truth until we have reached the full Bible standard again. If this be true, God will have to reform a sinful, corrupt leadership little by little, which is not His plan. Furthermore, such men will not be reformed. In God's plan the first step is to change man's heart and then change his head. Such leadership is described in II Tim. 3:1-8. "This know also, that in the last days perilous times shall come. (2) For men shall be lovers of their own selves, coveteous, boasters, proud, blasphemers, disobedient to parents, unthankful, unholy, (3) without natural affections, truce breakers, false accusers, incontinent, fierce, despisers of those that are good, (4) traitors, heady, highminded, lovers of pleasure more than lovers of God; (5) having a FORM OF GODLINESS, but denying the power thereof: from SUCH TURN AWAY. (6) For of THIS sort are they which creep into houses, and lead captive silly women laden with sins, led away with divers lusts, (7) EVER LEARNING, and NEVER able to come to the knowledge of the truth. (8) Now as Jannes and Jambres withstood Moses, SO DO THESE ALSO RESIST THE TRUTH: men of corrupt minds, reprobate concerning faith." These scriptures certainly apply to the time in which we live, called the "last days." Then he describes a very sinful, degraded, low class of people in religious circles, for he said: "Having a form of Godliness, but denying the power thereof." The non-professing world is not carrying on a form of godliness, but this is just what the people of Babylon are doing today. You only have to look around to find all these sins under the cover of religion. The leadership of Babylon has left the source of divine wisdom and knowledge and is streamlining the wisdom of men. In verse 7 we read, "Ever learning, and NEVER able to come to the knowledge of the truth." According to the above scripture there is NO TIME or PLACE where God can work a reform to bring such people to His standards of truth. These men are reprobate concerning the truth, and will resist it. This great battle of Armageddon, which we are now in, is led by the above described men against God and truth and will not REFORM.

Some tell us that when God said to "come out of Babylon," it was a call to the unsaved, non-professing world to get saved and come out of their sins. This is just another one of those excuses which the kings and captains use to justify their staying and hiding in "the dens and rocks" of the mountains of Babylon. The old devil, the enemy of all truth, scored a great hit when he succeeded in getting the people of the true Church of God to become lukewarm, spewed out, blinded to the truth that makes clear and sets forth a divine, holy people separate from the sins of Babylonian confusion. Many who have Church of God over their church door are in spirit and practice a part of "Babylon the Great." Some have no higher standards than Babylon herself. Union is Babylon's substitute for Bible unity. It is impossible to unite a multitude of corrupt things and make something pure, holy, and good. The spirit of union is the spirit of BABYLON THE GREAT—THE EIGHTH BEAST. The spirit of UNITY, based on the WORD OF GOD, is the SPIRIT OF TRUTH WHICH CAME FROM GOD. If reforming could eventually make the Church of God out of Babylon, it COULD NOT HAPPEN UNTIL ALL OF BABYLON WAS ELIMINATED AND LEFT BEHIND. Why suffer such a slow process when God has instant deliverance—just come out.

In the age in which we live, to have a CLEAR vision of Mt. Sion, we must have a vision of Babylon. The moment we see Mt. Sion we are in a position to exchange all our Babylonian traditions for God's glorious mountain of eternal TRUTH. If we are dead to the allurements of the Babylonian world, it will not be hard to walk out of it. Unless one is dead to the "lust of the flesh, the lust of the eye, and the pride of life" he will feel the price is too great to come out of Babylon, for she offers much to the satisfaction of the flesh.

Most all churches and movements have made laws and rules for the governing of their church machinery. This calls for a hierarchy of officers with offers to the lust of the flesh. It is contrary to the flesh to obey God's call and walk out. A LOVE for the truth is the only thing that will prompt such action. Many do not wish to "retain a love for the truth" and seek some excuse to remain in the rocks and hills of Babylon with a damnation resting on their souls.

The truth of the true church and Babylon is the sounding of "the great trumpet" spoken of in Isaiah 27 by which God said He would gather the outcasts of Israel and assemble them. This message concerning the true Church of God and Babylon is a part of the gospel and must go to all the world. Only those who are completely consecrated to the whole will of God, fully redeemed from all sin, and with the great LOVE OF GOD SHED ABROAD IN THEIR HEARTS BY THE HOLY GHOST, will be willing to be outcasts from the allurements of Babylon. "Lukewarm" people have lost their love for God and truth.

This great trumpet, the seventh and last in the gospel day, is clarifying truth as never before. We are urged to get back to the standards of the truth made clear in the past. Emphasis is laid on the language of the poem, "Back to the Blessed Old Bible." BABYLON THE GREAT, THE MOTHER OF HARLOTS, is clearly identified and her fornications are made clear before our eyes. The enticement of HER wine is clearly defined. The true brand of her merchandise is being stamped on her religious wares. Her institutions are being clarified as "Cages of unclean and hateful birds" and "a hold of foul spirits" working in its leadership. Multitudes upon multitudes have been spiritually martyred and lost their souls by accepting HER wares and drinking of the "wine of fornications." In the sounding of "the great trumpet" Babylon is being completely exposed. This is part of the gospel of God's great salvation that must reach all the world. Every one must be brought face to face with his OWN sin and deception. The responsibility of decision rests upon every individual. Groups may influence you, but the decision is an indivdual matter. Some will try to evade the responsibility through excuses and alibis, but God's justice demands that "Truth revealed must be answered to." Light rates responsibility! The greater the light the greater the responsibility. "At evening time it shall be light."

Individual responsibility is not to be pushed aside as though it was optional with the same reward. Of course, we have the privilege of accepting or refusing, but the eternal reward will be different.

In the sounding of this great and last trumpet the light of the gospel must go to all the world. All nations must hear God's full and complete message of gospel truth. This will bring the multitudes of the earth into the "Valley of Decision." Let us turn to the book of Joel, chapter 3, and see what he has to say about his valley.

"For behold, in those days, and in that time, when I shall bring AGAIN the captivity of Judah and Jerusalem, I will also gather all nations and will bring them down into the valley of Jehoshaphat, and will plead with them for my people and for my heritage Israel, whom they have scatterd among the nations and parted my land." We have already made it plain that we are living in that time when God is "bringing AGAIN" his people. In Isa. 11:11 it makes it clear that God is setting His hand AGAIN the second time to gather a remnant of his people. The fulfillment of Joel's prophecy is in this present age. At this time God is bringing all nations through the valley of decision, which the prophet Joel calls Jehoshaphat. The reason this valley is used is because of its location. It is nearby the City of Jerusalem. The gospel message when sounded out will bring the multitudes of the nations today into the valley of decision, drawing them near to the "heavenly Jerusalem." This is the valley of decision through which every one must come who hears God's message of truth. It is here that God PLEADS with those who are scattered in Babylon to return and be His people.

In verse 3, the prophet tells us what was done. "And they have cast lots for my people; and have given a boy for an harlot, and given a girl for wine, that they might drink." This shows us how the kings and captains in Babylon have traded and commercialized on the souls of boys and girls, selling them for the wine of Babylon's fornication.

In verse 4 we read, "Yea, and what have ye to do with me, O Tyre, and Zidon, and all the coasts of Palestine?" Some people try to run and get away from God, but this is one VALLEY all must come through. God said He would gather all nations into this place and plead with them. Wherever the full gospel message of God's truth is preached, people are forced through this valley. God pleads with people to return and recompense Him, that he may recompense them.

Verse 5, "Because ye have taken my silver and my gold, and have carried into your temples (Babylon) my goodly pleasant things: (Verse 6) The children also of Judah and the children of Jerusalem have ye sold unto the Grecians, that ye might remove them far from their border. (Verse 7) Behold, I will raise them out of the place whither ye have sold them, and will return your recompense upon your own heads. (Verse 8) And I will sell your sons and daughters into the hands of the children of Judah, and they shall sell them unto Sebeans, to a people far off: for the Lord hath spoken it."

The spirit of Grecia conquered God's people and carried them into Babylon during the dark and cloudy day. They took the silver and gold and all the goodly things down into their Babylonian temples. Then in verse 8, God said he would sell their sons and daughters back to Judah. Judah represents the remnant of God's people which he gathered out on Mt. Sion in the sixth seal. Then he says they sold them back again into the hands of the Sebeans. At the close of the sixth seal, those who had been the people of God, compromised and let down the standards again. Selling themselves to the Sabeans means selling themselves into the idol worship of Babylon. This brings us down to the time of the seventh seal and the sounding of the great trumpet. We will read Joel 3:9 and see what he says to do. "Proclaim ye this among the Gentiles: Proclaim war, wake up the mighty men, let all the men of war draw near; let them come up." This brings us once more to the great battle of Armageddon. He said to proclaim this among the Gentiles, or the Babylonian world. God is calling for every soldier of the cross to step into the ranks of battle. It is time for the mighty men to wake up and come up. Come out of the hills of Babylon and climb God's Mt. Sion of truth.

Joel 3:10 tells us what to do: "Beat your plowshares into swords and your pruning hooks into spears: let the weak say, I am strong." In Isaiah 2:4 this scripture is reversed. He says, "Beat your swords into plowshares and your spears into pruning hooks." Isaiah was speaking to the church in the morning time when the hearts of men could be plowed and pruned and would bring forth fruit unto God. But it is different today; people have become gospel hardened. There are those in Babylon who will not hear God's message of truth. God has promised vengeance on Babylon. He is calling them into the valley of Jehoshaphat, pleading with them to accept His last call back to his standards of truth. He offers life for death, and truth for error. God's message of truth against the sins of Babylon no longer needs to be guessed at. It is a savor unto life or death. God's message is like the sword and spear—it kills. We must die to the sins of Babylon or die in them. In this manner the message of God on the soul is likened unto a sword and a spear on the body.

In this great trumpet, which is being blown today, it sounds a message of salvation to the heathen world. They, too, will be gathered into the valley of decision. This great trumpet will be heard by all classes of people. It will sound out the needs of every man with a pleading invitation for its acceptance.

The picture of this great spiritual battle of Armageddon, fought in the valley of Jehoshaphat near the heavenly Jerusalem, is changed into a HARVEST field. "Put ye in the sickle, for the harvest is ripe: come, get you down; for the press is full, the vats overflow; for their wickedness is great. Multitudes, multitudes in the valley of decision: for the day of the Lord is near in valley of decision." Joel 3:13, 14.

The Word of God is the sickle. Its complete message is going to all nations, bringing them into the valley of Jehoshaphat, showing them the glorious divine Church of God on one side of the valley, and Babylon and the world on the other side. The kind of decision made will determine the location of the multitudes, as they go to the place of their choosing. Those who see God's great salvation and His glorious Church, and are WILLING TO WALK IN THE LIGHT, will ascend Mt. Sion and enter THE HEAVENLY JERUSALEM. The wheat is being gathered into the garner, a place of safety and security inside the walls of truth. The chaff, those who reject and refuse the truth, are gathered into the fire and burned with the judgments of God's eternal truth.

In Matt. 13:3 Jesus gives us a parable of the sower. "Behold a sower went forth to sow." He gives us four kinds of soil, telling of four classes of people, represented by the wayside, the stony places, the thorns, and thistles.

In Matt. 13:24-30 Jesus gives us another parable of His kingdom, which extends through the entire gospel day. "Another parable put he forth unto them, saying; the kingdom of heaven is likened unto a man which sowed good seed in his field (the entire world): but while men slept, his enemy came and sowed tares among the wheat, and went his way. But when the blades were sprung up, and brought forth fruit, then appeared the tares also. So the servants of the householder came and said unto him, Sir, didst not thou sow good seed in thy field? from whence then hath it tares? He said unto them, an enemy hath done this. The servants said unto him, Wilt thou then that we go and gather them up? But he said, Nay; lest while ye gather up the tares, ye root also the wheat with them. Let them grow together until the harvest: and in the time of harvest, I will say to the reapers, gather ye together first the tares, and bind them in bundles to burn them: but gather the wheat into my barn."

Now in verses 37 to 41, Jesus gives us an explanation of this parable. "He that soweth the good seed is the Son of man; the field is the world; the good seed are the children of the kingdom; but the tares are the children of the wicked one; the enemy that sowed them is the devil; the harvest is the end of the world; and the reapers are the angels (ministers). The Son of man (Jesus) shall send forth his angels (His ministers) and they shall gather out of his kingdom all things (people) that offend, and them which do iniquity."

Now let us get a picture of the kingdom extending through the entire world or gospel day, and the Son of man sowing the good seed through His servants. While men slept spiritually through the dark and cloudy day, the devil sowed the seed that developed the wickedness of Babylon. Through the middle ages and even until yet, the good and the bad, the saved and the unsaved, have grown together inside the walls of Babylon.

God did not see fit to send judgment on Babylon during the dark and cloudy day, and separate the good from the bad at that time. He said, "Let them grow together until the harvest," and the harvest is in the end of the world. Jesus said, "Say not four months, then cometh the harvest," but open your eyes, for the harvest is already ripe. The harvesting of souls into the kingdom has always been ripe since the kingdom was preached in the early ages of the church, but the harvest at the end of the world is a separating time. This seventh trumpet message, which Isaiah said was a great trumpet, is shaking the Babylonian nations and the Church, with a message that brings them into the valley of decision. If they decide against God's message of truth, they are gathered out of the kingdom. Some will offend at some minor point of truth and will be guilty before God. Let us remember that it is our own decision that causes us to be removed out of the kingdom. This responsibility is a personal and individual matter. We are told that the results of preaching God's message will be as stated in verse 42. "And shall cast them into a furnace of fire;

there shall be weeping and gnashing of teeth." The Holy Spirit fire burns the souls of every one that rebels against truth. The wailing and gnashing of teeth will begin now, but will last forever.

There will only be a remnant left in the kingdom. Not many are willing to be freed from Babylonian bondage. They would rather stay with the crowds. Many are hunting hiding places in the holes and dens of the rocks and mountains of Babylon, trying to shield themselves from the "furnace of fire."

In Matt. 13:43 Jesus shows us the visibility of the righteous: "Then shall the righteous shine forth as the sun in the kingdom of their Father." God still has a few who are not hunting any holes or hiding places. With sword and spear in hand they have ascended Mt. Sion. With the "great trumpet" to their lips they are sounding a blast of truth that is shaking Babylon to pieces, and is testing every man's work.

"Now if any man build upon this foundation gold, silver, precious stone, wood, hay, stubble; every man's work shall be made manifest: for the day shall declare it, because it shall be revealed by fire; and the fire shall try every man's work of what sort it is. If any man's work abide which he hath built thereupon, he shall receive a reward. If any man's work shall be burned, he shall suffer loss; but he himself shall be saved, yet so as by fire." I Cor. 3:12-17.

It is certain that Christ is the only foundation on which to build. Paul has just told us that there are two kinds of works: the perishable and the unperishable. The gold, silver, and precious stones represent truth, and it will not burn. The Holy Spirit fire will never affect it. All man-made theories and doctrines are classed as wood, hay, and stubble. These are all combustible and are being destroyed by the fires of God's holiness and truth.

There have been many saved people in the past who, without knowledge, built with wood, hay, and stubble. With the blood of Christ having been applied to their souls, and God having winked at their ignorance, they were saved by the fire of God's justice, but their works are all being burned in the judgment fires of his truth. Honest souls, who love God and His truth with all their hearts, will be sorry when they see their mistakes and will rejoice at its destruction by the fire of truth.

If the binding in bundles, spoken of by Jesus in His parable, has any spiritual significance in spiritual things, it would mean that everything was bound in its own class and kind, and burned by the fire and truth that destroyed it.

God is clearing His kingdom of those who are seed on stony ground and among thorns and thistles. Every mans' stability is tested and tried. His love, consecration and endurance is tested. God is not pleased with those who cannot stand the scorching fires of the Sun of righteousness which will only cleanse and purify. It will be only a small part, a remnant, that will stand the test. With God, quality is preferred before quantity and great numbers. God has a remnant in the ministry, filled with love, power, and victory — "Redeemed from among men" and "Not defiled with women," man-made churches. They are kindling the fire of Holy Spirit judgment and truth which will destroy everything that is wood, hay, and stubble.

This gospel MUST be preached to all the world; all MUST come through the great valley of truth, with a decision to make. This TRUTH becomes a sickle in the hands of the angels, the ministry, whom God said he would send. The decision each individual MUST make determines whether they are to become "wheat for the garner" or "chaff for the furnace of fire."

Let us notice the blessed condition of those gathered into this garner of SOUL REST, SAFETY, AND SECURITY. In Rev. 14:10-11 we are shown the torments of those who worshipped the beast and his image with the smoke of their torment ascending up for ever and ever. These torments begin as people come out on the wrong side of the valley of decision, and will never end. In verse 12 we are told that this is a time when the saints will have need of patience, but verse 13 tells us of the blessedness of their condition. "And I heard a voice from heaven saying unto me, Write, Blessed are the dead which die in the Lord from henceforth (or from now on); yea, saith the Spirit, that they may rest from their labors, and their works do follow them."

This is trying to teach us a spiritual lesson. This dying in the Lord is spiritual. It will take a complete dying to ALL THINGS to get out on the right side of this valley of decision. This is called dying in the Lord. From this time on, they may rest from their carnal labors of perishable things. But their works of righteousness do follow them. Those who can walk out on the side of God's heavenly Jerusalem, and claim God's Mt. Sion of light and truth, refusing to obey the voice of the enemy and those who make the wrong decisions, certainly are blessed of God. It takes dead people to do this.

At the sounding of this seventh trumpet and last message ALL immediately emerge into the valley of DECISION. The great Holy Spirit firmly fixes the TRUTH to be decided upon on the heart and soul of the listener, forcing them into the valley of decision. There is no alternative. All must face the issue. Only a few came out on God's side.

In Rev. 14:14-16, John tells us of a white cloud and the Son of man sitting on it with a sharp sickle in his hand. This once more points us to the harvest Jesus said would be in the end of the world. In these verses we are told that the earth was reaped, which has reference to the earthly originated doctrines of men.

In verse 17 we see this sickle in the hands of an angel coming out of the temple, which would mean the ministry of the church now has the message. This message is the sounding of the seventh or last trumpet to the nations. In verse 18 we see another angel or ministry which has power over fire. It says that they came out from the altar. There are a few ministers who linger at the altar until they are endowed with fire that will burn up the chaff while the wheat is being gathered into the garner. The message of this angel was, "Thrust in thy sharp sickle, and gather the clusters of the vine of the earth; for her grapes are fully ripe. And the angel thrust in his sickle into the earth, and gathered the vine of the earth, and cast it into the great winepress of the wrath of God. And the winepress was trodden without the city, and blood came out of the winepress, even unto the horse bridles, by the space of a thousand and six hundred furlongs." Rev. 14:18-20.

Here we have the harvesting of the cluster of the vine of the earth. In St. John 15, Jesus said, "I am the TRUE vine." This is the harvesting of the false vine, which is the cluster of Babylonian doctrines and institutions. This is that harvest that Jesus said would be "in the end of the world." The fullnes of the cluster of the vine of all man-made institutions is being cast into the "winepress of the wrath of God." This winepress was "trodden without" the city or beyond the city limits of Babylon. Even there, judgment was laid to the line, so that all may understand it. The last part of verse 20 seems to imply a battlefield which alludes to the battle of "Armageddon." This is taken from ancient warfare when they rode horses into battle. The rider is responsible for the use of the reins or bits of the bridle, and his "blood" is upon his own shoulders.

In the "valley of Jehoshaphat" we have a combination of TYPES, SHADOWS and SYMBOLS, having their spiritual fulfillment in the time in which we are living. The old prophet told us in Joel 3:1 that it would be "In those days, and in that time, WHEN I SHALL BRING AGAIN THE CAPTIVITY OF JUDAH AND JERUSALEM, I will also gather all nations . . . into the valley of Jehoshaphat." This is the age in which God is setting His hand again the second time to gather a remnant of his people. Isa. 11:11.

Three things are happening in this symbolical valley of "evening light" and truth. The first thing to be done on entering this valley is to make a DECISION. On one side is the city of Babylon, scattered on the hills of confusion. Her kings and captains with vain promises and fair speeches are offering her religious wares. Much of her merchandise offers to the satisfying of the lust of the flesh, the lust of the eye, and the pride of life. She has much to offer to the "lovers of pleasure." The upper seats in the synagogues have their appeal to those who love the praise and applause of men. No one is required to be spiritual; that is old-fashioned and out of date. The minister is offered many opportunities with chance for promotion if he can sell the goods. For success in this, the preacher invokes God's blessings upon them, with a bogus promise that they will have an abundant entrance into the celestial city at the end. These things can be plainly seen by every one who enters the valley of God's glorious truth.

As we enter this valley, the glorious light and truth illuminates our souls as never before. Prophetic and symbolic mysteries dazzle our spiritual eyes with a seven-fold brightness. The hungry, sincere, honest souls will begin to feast on food they did not know existed. Before us is God's glorious Mt. Sion, His heavenly Jerusalem, THE GLORIOUS CHURCH OF GOD, free from all sin, sectarianism and man-rule. Jesus Christ is her Head, Governor, and Ruler. In all things He is given "preeminence." God's people know their needs. God's promises are plain before them that He will supply them. They are standing on the faith line of victory with signs and miracles following their ministry.

As we step into this valley of light and truth, and look at the results of decision, we see a great harvest time. Many who see light on God's Word and do not retain a love for truth, are offended and turn to the hills of Babylon, believing a delusion with damnation resting on their souls. If they were saved they were in the kingdom, but when they are offended at even one point of truth, they are gathered out of His kingdom. Jesus wants a clean church and only those on clean soil. He wants those among thorns and thistles and on stony ground put to a test and gathered out of His kingdom, that those on good ground "May shine as the sun in the kingdom of their Father." You do not have to know all the Word of God to become responsible before God. Each one is responsible for what he knows, let it be much or little. Some dump the whole thing overboard because they do not understand some parts of it. This will not excuse you for that part you understand when you stand at the final judgment.

Those on good ground love God with all their heart, soul, mind, and strength, and "nothing offends them." They accept all the truth they understand, and are ready for the rest when it comes. Their eyes are set toward the top of Mt. Sion. They hunger and thirst for the fullness of God's trtuh. They are dead to Babylon and her allurements, and are never satisfied until they reach the top of glorious Mt.

Sion, and there pitch their tent in "the camp of the saints," and launch their little barks on the great river which Isaiah said "would flow in the top of the mountain."

This is the time of harvest at the end of the world. If you cannot pass the one hundred percent test of purity, holiness, and goodness according to your own decision, you will be numbered with the tares and burned as chaff in the furnace of Holy Spirit fire.

Now let us change this scene in this valley of Jehoshaphat and view it as the great battle of Armageddon. This is not a literal battle as some would have us believe. Most all of the prophecies of the prophets pointing to the gospel day, the parable of Jesus, and the symbolic language of the book of Revelation must be given a spiritual interpretation. To literalize them would destroy the kingdom that Jesus came to set up, which is a kingdom of righteousness, joy and peace in the Holy Ghost.

In this valley of decision is where soldiers enlist for the battle. You will never be drafted, but you will be forced to say, yes or no. The devil will tell you not to do it, that you can't make it, and if you do, it will not pay. The devil will further magnify the hardships of a soldier of the cross. He will send his angels with flowery speeches of discouragement. He will tell you that you can never accomplish anything with those few outcasts.

But the voice of the Holy Spirit can be heard in this valley, for here is where He talks. This is where He pleads with the nations. He, too, will show you the hardships of a soldier of the cross. He will lay before you standards and requirements which you must meet. The plain, unmistakable word will be heard, "Follow thou Me." He will further tell us not to be ashamed of Him or His words, and take up our cross and follow Him. It will be made very clear that we will be criticized, persecuted, and reviled for the stand we take concerning this full gospel message of evening light truth. The final test is—He brings us to a LIFE and DEATH consecration. He died for us. We must be willing to die for the sake of His truth.

This great battle of Armageddon is fought between the forces of God's saints gathered out on Mt. Sion and the forces of Babylon. In this great valley of decision is where people choose which side they are on. It is folly for one to believe he can work for God and remain on the devil's side, but to walk out is wisdom's way. This valley of evening light and truth makes it clear and you make the choice as to what side you are on. When light comes to a saved person in Babylon, and they see the glorious Church of God, they CANNOT remain in Babylon and stay saved. While some feel that they can do some good by staying there, how can a person be worth anything to the cause of God, or any one else, in a backslidden condition? God's message is: "Come out of her, my people, that ye be not partakers of her sins," and the message bearers should practice what they preach.

It is true that Babylon has some good hung on the outside. She has taken some of the "precious things" and decked the outside, but inwardly she is full of adulterous abominations. All saved people have some truth, but when you come out of Babylon, bring what truth you have, but be sure you do not bring with you some of your old Babylon clothes and practices.

This great battle is fought with a loss and gain on both sides. When one side gains or captures a man, of course the other side loses him. While some are being disfellowshipped and turned out of Babylon for preaching the truth of God's Word, there are others who see the abominations of Babylon, and the glorious Church of God, and come out of their own accord. There are some who seem to run well for a time, but after a while selfish motives revive, they make a compromise deal with the devil, and are captured by his forces. All it takes to be a part of Babylon is to adopt Babylonian practices. What it takes to be the real Mt. Sion Church of God is to be governed by the Word and the Spirit. The Word and the Spirit always agree. The wrong spirit will not agree with the right interpretation, and the wrong interpretation will not agree with the Holy Spirit.

There are some who see all the abominations of Babylon. They visualize her unscriptural foundations and operations. They see her sins, deceptions, graft, and hypocrisies. Discouraged, cast down and soul sick, they decide to get out of religion and quit professing to be anything. Such a one is standing in the valley of decision, but he sees only the abominations of Babylon. They need to hear the gospel which will make plain God's great plan of complete redemption for a lost world. Then they need to see God's redeemed host walking in the light, and climbing God's Mt. Sion of truth, coming to the unity of the faith. They need to see a group of people of which Jesus is the head, and whom the Holy Spirit is leading and directing, because He is dwelling in their hearts. In such a group they can see holiness, victory, power, and glory with signs following, because they believe and practice ALL the Word of God. In such a group can be seen a sweet spirit, and a love for all men, but no love for Babylonian practices. Surely a vision of the privilege of becoming a particular member in that church which Jesus owns and recognizes as His Bride, with His great loving arms of protection and care thrown around her, is sufficient to win the affections of the soul of those who want the real love and affection of the Master.

Some come out of Babylon and start, or enter, another part of Babylon as bad or worse than the one they came out of, hoping to be the head of it. To come out of Babylon is not enough. God has something for us to come to. "But ye are come unto Mt. Sion, and unto the city of the living God, the heavenly Jerusalem and to an innumerable company of angels, to the general assembly and church of the first born, which are written in heaven, and to God, the Judge of all, and to the spirits of just men made perfect, and to Jesus the mediator of the new covenant, and to the blood of sprinkling that speaketh better things than that of Abel." Heb. 12:22-24.

It will not be hard to identify the true church of God when we see a people on the Bible foundations, preaching and practicing all the Bible, bearing the fruits of the Spirit, manifesting all the gifts of the Spirit, and with the signs following that Jesus said would follow them that believe. God is not satisfied with less than this, and we should not be satisfied until we have reached that goal. Only those who live under the drippings of God's sanctuary of holiness, power, and wisdom will be able to discern the devil's substitutes and imitations. The devil has power to perform miracles. In Moses' time, Aaron's rod was turned to a serpent in the presence of Pharoah. He sent for the wise men and their rods also were turned into serpents. We notice that Aaron's serpent swallowed theirs. This shows us that God is the greater power.

The devil is working his miracles in modern Babylon today. He has his substitutes for the gifts of the Spirit and the signs that Jesus said would follow them that believe. Through these false manifestations and demonstrations he is deceiving many, who are looking for something more than dead, lifeless formality. These demonstrations carry a close resemblance of the real Bible signs and gifts.

Some times it takes discernment, a close examination and testing with Bible truth. I am persuaded that all the serpents in Aaron's time looked alike, but the final test showed which one was of God.

The devil has his false holy ghost, with his false evidence of speaking in tongues, which makes people powerless and helpless, but causes them to do things which are not decent nor becoming. The power that God gives causes people to stand upright, bear the fruit of the Spirit, and testify intelligently to what God has done.

If there are those present who cannot understand the speaker's language, God may give the gift of "tongues" or speaking in other languages, so that the speaker may speak and testify in their own language the great things of God. This is not a sign to the one speaking that he has the Holy Ghost, but a sign to the unbeliever, when he hears the wonderful message of God. I Cor. 14:22. When the wrong spirit gets hold of people, it makes them demonstrate and do things they would not do otherwise. I have seen them shake, quiver and fall, kick and roll, and act very unbecoming with their face drawn into a Satanic look, slobber and make noises. This, they said, was speaking in tongues. The most of this noise was not any language at all. Usually it consists of a lingo of a few different sounds repeated over and over. Some times the devil has his interpreter there, who would interpret these certain sounds to mean many different things.

The devil has his miracles and healings. If the devil could make a serpent out of a rod, he can heal a sick person in order to deceive them. I have seen those who said they had the gift of healing, but only had the devil's deception. When they prayed for one sick, they would fall powerless on the floor. Sometimes they get up and walk in a miraculous way, but with some peculiar look on their face or some actions that are foreign to the Spirit of God. Some of these great healers have peculiar actions while performing these miracles. They roll their eyes and look wild. It is plain to see that some power gets hold of them. Sometimes they treat the sick person very rough, shake them unmercifully, and slap them with their hand. When the power strikes the one being prayed for, there is a peculiar Satanic look on their face. I have seen the false and I have seen the real. The contrast is outstanding. They act different, look different and manifest a different spirit.

I have talked with individuals who acknowledged they were not even saved, were immoral characters, yet they could speak this false tongue. I have seen those who were convinced that they had a false spirit, acknowledged it as unscriptural, wanted to get rid of it, and have the devils cast out.

The devil is using these signs and wonders to deceive people and get them away from the real thing. God gets no glory out of the devil's work, even though it is done in His name. Some honest people are led into this deception because they do not examine it close enough to detect the source from which it comes. If saved people would earnestly pray for God to keep them from going into anything displeasing to Him, and would reject every appearance of deception as fast as it comes, they would not be led into the devil's traps. God says to try the spirits. We must put them to a Biblical test. If they are wrong, we must take a firm stand in our hearts against them and rebuke them in the name of the Lord.

In this little book I have tried to show what Babylon is and what it is not. I am acknowledging that she has carried some of the good things of God down into her domain, but God said, "Your silver and your gold will not save you in the day of His wrath and judgment," and His message is, "Come out of her, my people, be not partakers of her sins." It seems clear to me that any honest and fair-minded person can see what Babylon is, and what God says to do about it.

I have tried to describe Babylon in plain language, backed by the Word of God. I have not intended to say harsh things about any person or group of people, but I have done my best to expose things and conditions that surround them. I carry no ill will or malice against any religious people, even those of the lowest type and kind. I have a love that would reach for the lowest and lift them to the highest, if they would only let God do it. I have felt the presence, power, and approval of God as I write. Many times I have lifted my heart to the God of all creation, and asked Him somehow to awake and bless the fallen and sleeping nations.

I send this little book out with a prayer from the depth of my soul that its readers will not only see Babylon, but also see the great, grand, and glorious New Testament Mt. Sion Church of God, the heavenly Jerusalem, in her splendor and glory as John saw her "adorned as a bride for her husband." AMEN AND AMEN.

OTHER BOOKS BY THE AUTHOR

The Three Temples
The Reformation
Answers to Prayer of Faith
The Seven Churches of Asia
Redemption Through Christ

J. F. Lawson, P. D. Turnbow and D. W. Rogers are co-authors of Revelation with Gospel and Prophecy, Revised.

The above books may be obtained as long as they last by writing to: P. D. TURNBOW, Moore, Okla.

All offerings will be used for the Lord's work.

CPSIA information can be obtained
at www.ICGtesting.com
Printed in the USA
FFOW01n1812190515
13419FF